PENGUIN BOOKS

HELGA'S DIARY

Helga Weiss was born in Prague in 1929. Her father, Otto, was employed in the state bank in Prague and her mother, Irena, was a dressmaker. Of the 15,000 children brought to Terezín and later deported to Auschwitz, only 100 survived the Holocaust. Helga was one of them. On her return to Prague she studied art and has become well known for her paintings. The drawings and paintings that Helga made during her time in Terezín, which accompany this diary, were published in 1998 in the book *Draw What You See* (*Zeichne, was Du siehst*). Her father's novel *And God saw that it was bad*, written during his time in Terezín and which she illustrated, was published in 2010. In 1954 Helga married the musician Jiří Hošek. She has two children, three grandchildren and lives to this day in the flat where she was born.

Helga's Diary

A Young Girl's Account of Life in a Concentration Camp

HELGA WEISS

Translated by Neil Bermel

PENGUIN BOOKS

PENGUIN BOOKS

Published by the Penguin Group
Penguin Books Ltd, 80 Strand, London WC2R ORL, England
Penguin Group (USA) Inc., 375 Hudson Street, New York, New York 10014, USA
Penguin Group (Canada), 90 Eglinton Avenue East, Suite 700, Toronto, Ontario, Canada M4P 2Y3
(a division of Pearson Penguin Canada Inc.)
Penguin Ireland, 25 St Stephen's Green, Dublin 2, Ireland
(a division of Penguin Books Ltd)
Penguin Group (Australia), 707 Collins Street, Melbourne, Victoria 3008, Australia
(a division of Pearson Australia Group Pty Ltd)
Penguin Books India Pvt Ltd, 11 Community Centre,
Panchsheel Park, New Delhi – 110 017, India
Penguin Group (NZ), 67 Apollo Drive, Rosedale, Auckland 0632, New Zealand
(a division of Pearson New Zealand Ltd)
Penguin Books (South Africa) (Pty) Ltd, Block D, Rosebank Office Park,
181 Jan Smuts Avenue, Parktown North, Gauteng 2193, South Africa

Penguin Books Ltd, Registered Offices: 80 Strand, London WC2R ORL, England

www.penguin.com

First published by Viking 2013
Published in Penguin Books 2014
005

Text copyright © Helga Weiss, 2013
Translation copyright © Neil Bermel, 2013
Paintings copyright © Wallstein Verlag, 1998
The Illustration Credits on pages 225–6 constitute an extension of this copyright page
All rights reserved

The moral right of the copyright holders has been asserted

Maps drawn by Michael Hill at Maps Illustrated

A shortened version of the diary of Helga Weiss was included in the book *Deníky dětí* (*Children's Diaries*), published by
Naše vojsko (Our Armed Forces) in 1961, and in the book *Terezín*, which was published by the Council of Jewish
Communities in the Czech Lands in Prague in 1965. Quotations from the diary were also used in several documentaries,
such as Zuzana Justmanová's 1997 film *Voices of the Children*

Typeset by Palimpsest Book Production Limited, Falkirk, Stirlingshire
Printed in Great Britain by Clays Ltd, St Ives plc

ISBN: 978–0–241–95950–3

www.greenpenguin.co.uk

To my granddaughters, Dominika, Natálie and Sarah, and to all young people, in the hope that they will keep the past alive in their memories, and that they will never experience for themselves what my generation has had to live through.

Contents

Translator's Note

Helga's surviving manuscripts consist of two stapled school notebooks and a stack of paper that she used once the notebooks ran out. Over the years, she worked on them several times, writing over and into her original scripts in pencil and making several revised versions of them, one an early typescript that survives as well.

Although the current edition presents Helga's journals as a daily diary, according to her wishes, the original composition of the work is more varied.

~

The notebooks
The surviving notebooks recount Helga's time in Prague and later at Terezín internment camp. Textual evidence shows that she did not keep daily entries; instead, she picked up the journal at greater intervals and wrote long entries covering months at a stretch. This explains in part what would have been an uncanny awareness of the significance of events, as well as accounting for the occasional chronological hiccup, when two events close in time are transposed in order.

The first notebook begins with a reminiscence about Helga's 'childhood' (remember that at the time she started writing she was a child herself, certainly no older than fourteen) and continues by recounting scenes and events from the early wartime years, documented in a mixture of past and present narration. The narrative style is, with the exception of the first few pages, remarkably consistent, with Helga telling her stories as if she is reliving them just moments later.

In the current edition, which follows a version of the text that Helga put together after the war, she has rewritten the passages about 1938 and the first half of 1939, stripping out some of her childish purple prose and putting them in a format more like that of the remaining sections, and she has added dates throughout the work. Although these now read like daily diary entries, therefore, they were not originally so. This explains the maturity of the style, which would have been highly improbable for a child of eight or nine.

Helga edited the text of the notebooks after the war as she made her typescript version. In her edits, Helga has removed some comments and episodes that perhaps seemed to her overly critical of people (who were possibly still alive at that point) and cut down some of the discursive and repetitive episodes that she felt were of little interest. This editing has been retained at Helga's express wishes, so what readers have in front of them is the post-war version, rather than the text of the original notebooks. Roughly a quarter of the notebooks' text was excised, and a further quarter underwent some stylistic editing. In a few places, Helga added further observations after the war, and these have been signalled in the endnotes.

Helga's second notebook ends with an entry concerning the family's arrival at Terezín in 1941 and their separation. This was apparently written in 1943, as in the notebook Helga says she remembers this scene 'even now, two years later'.

⌀

The loose-leaf papers

What survives in manuscript form from after that date are individual sheets of paper, some possibly written down while she was at the camp and many others written after the war. At this point, we can only take educated guesses as to which pages date from when, based on the paper itself and the handwriting. Here, more than in the notebooks, substantial editing is visible right on the manuscript pages. Because the pages were not numbered or dated, as they got misfiled and reshuffled over the years, the original order was lost. Furthermore, when Helga was writing and editing her work after the war, reference works about the Holocaust were few and far between, so rather than working to a strict chronology, she often wrote and grouped entries thematically. For example, where she had mentioned a cultural event, she included the names of one or two others that she attended later as well.

Some research and interpretation was thus needed to put this section into an order that made sense, without traducing what was on the original pages. In translating this section, I have used Helga's authorized, edited text, and have as far as possible followed the ordering in that text. However, in some places I have placed entries in a different order from Helga's original guesses, as long as in doing so I was able to respect the composition of the original manuscripts. Some discrepancies remain, due to the thematic way in which the entries were composed, but notes will direct readers to many of the remaining issues with the timeline of events.

⌐

The remaining text

The final section of the diary is similarly written in diary format, but was composed necessarily, as Helga explains in her Preface, on her return to Prague after the war during 1945 and 1946. There is no surviving manuscript of this section, so it relies entirely on the post-war typescript. The composition of it is still in diary form, continuing in the same vein as Helga had done in her wartime account. In our interview (see page 188), Helga explains why she wrote this third section in the format of a diary.

⌐

The translation and the format

In my translation, I have tried to respect Helga's vision of a text that is readable for modern sensibilities while keeping to her authorized version. This is not a definitive scholarly edition, and my own changes to the text have thus been minimal. The gaps, awkward bits, jumps and repetitions are there to begin with, and it's our job as modern readers to try to bridge the gulf between our world and Helga's childhood world.

For this reason, readers will find notes at the back to explain some of the references that Helga would have taken for granted. In very occasional places, I have inserted an extra explanatory word or two into the main text to make a reference point clear, but for the most part these references are explained in the notes. Helga's original paragraphs are often very long, so in places I have taken the liberty of breaking them in two to offer readers a pause between thoughts.

Helga wrote her journal as an adolescent and, as is understandable for a child living in dramatic times, she mentioned dates only occasionally. Dates as entry headings appear first sporadically, as later insertions on some of the loose-leaf pages, and are not found consistently until the post-war typescript; these were thus inserted retrospectively as best as Helga could recall or figure out after the war.

We have left Helga's reconstructed dates as an aid to readers, but rather than try to add further dates throughout the text, which would be well nigh impossible, we have attempted to forestall confusion in readers' minds, as Helga switches tenses and subjects, with two further sorts of break within the text. A larger gap with a scroll (⌒) indicates the beginning of a fresh episode in the diary, the introduction of a new subject or concern, often but not necessarily preceded by a larger, or at least a definite, passage of time. A small gap with a star (*) simply indicates that some time may have passed between paragraphs, perhaps only a few hours, perhaps a couple of days, but the subject remains the same and the narrative is essentially continuous. These gaps do not correspond to gaps in the original manuscript, and should not be taken to indicate that Helga has put her diary down and returned to it afresh.

Similarly, the diary is presented here in three parts – the first covers her experiences in Prague, the second her time in Terezín and the third her experiences thereafter – but readers should know that these divisions are not original to the text.

I have followed Helga in citing place names in Czech, unless there is a common English version, such as Prague, or unless the German name is more familiar. Sometimes, as in the case of Brüx–Most, she uses both terms, in which case I have stuck with the modern Czech place name so as not to confuse readers.

Helga's Diary contains a number of German words that describe places and activities in the camps. As she wrote in Czech and it was her native tongue, I've preserved many of these interlopers to give a flavour of the original. Czech readers of today would struggle with these alien words if anything more than English speakers do. Some readers may find it strange that frequently a German word is mixed with an English ending (*Krankenträgers*, meaning 'stretcher-bearers'). This again reflects the original text, in which Helga increasingly incorporates the official language of the camp – German – into her own language, adapting it to the flective demands of her native Czech. In many places, however, I have provided a translation or explanation in English so as not to disrupt readers too greatly. A short German glossary can be found at the end of the text that contains many of the more frequent German words Helga uses. (Helga and I discussed some of these words in greater detail in her interview.)

Many of the places mentioned in the book are, of course, still there to this day and can be visited. Terezín, designated by the Germans as a transit camp for Jews to be deported to labour and extermination camps elsewhere in the Reich, and later tarted up to claim to the international community that the Jews were being treated humanely, is a Czech national monument. The Trade Fair Palace, a 1920s building in the northern Prague suburb of Holešovice, is now an art gallery belonging to the National Gallery (although the Radio Palace next door, where the actual internments took place, has been knocked down; a plaque, designed by Helga, marks its location). And other camps where Helga was interned, such as Auschwitz-Birkenau and Mauthausen, are open to the public as well.

Helga, incidentally, still lives in the flat where she was born and where the opening events of her journal take place.

Acknowledgments

In preparing this translation, I had recourse to many sources, including the official websites of the Terezín National Monument, the educational portal Holocaust.cz, the Vedem project, the United States Holocaust Memorial Museum, the YIVO encyclopedia, the Prague Jewish Museum, the town of Terezín, the Czech National Gallery, the Prague Information Service, Mauthausen Memorial, Czech Radio and the Terezín Initiative Institute. The websites www.ghetto-theresienstadt.info, www.fronta.cz, www. jewishgen.org and vysocina-news.cz were further important sources. Other interviews on the web with Holocaust survivors provided valuable context and corroborating information, such as those on www.hermanova.de, www.holocaustresearchproject. org, historycz.edublogs.org and www.holocaustcenterbuff.com.

Among the books I consulted were Hans Günther Adler's *Theresienstadt: das Antlitz einer Zwangsgemeinschaft*, Norbert Troller's *Theresienstadt: Hitler's Gift to the Jews*, *The Terezin Diary of Gonda Redlich* (ed. Saul Friedman and trans. Laurence Kutler), Joža Karas's *Music in Terezín, 1941–45*, Alena Heitlinger's *In the*

Shadows of the Holocaust and Communism: Czech and Slovak Jews since 1945 and Pokoj 127, a memoir by six Terezín survivors, Tom Luke, Mordechaj Livni, Chava Livni, Petr Herrmann, Eva Ročková and Jan Roček.

I'm also grateful to Edgar de Bruin for his invaluable collaboration in reconstructing the chronology of the diary; to Luděk Knittl for his linguistic assistance; to Andrew Swartz for his moral support; and to the UK editor, Will Hammond, for his patient and assured shepherding of this project from beginning to end.

Neil Bermel
Sheffield University, 2012

Maps

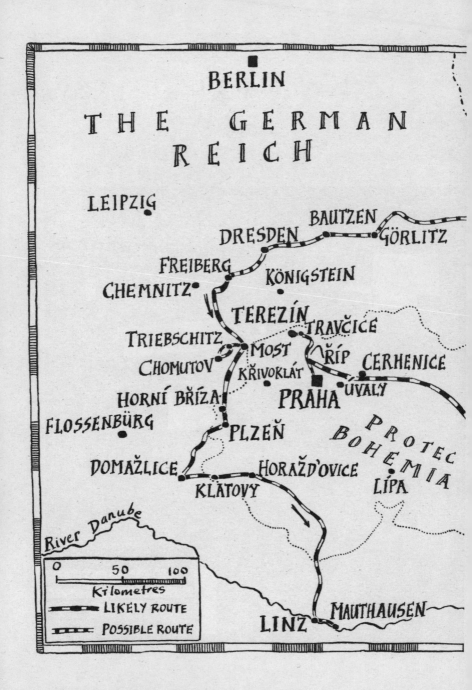

HELGA'S JOURNEY

WARSAW

THE GENERAL GOVERNMENT OF POLAND
(OCCUPIED BY GERMAN REICH)

BRESLAU

KATOWICE

CRACOW

BIRKENAU

AUSCHWITZ

TORATE OF & MORAVIA

OSTRAVA

BRNO

SLOVAKIA

VIENNA

HUNGARY

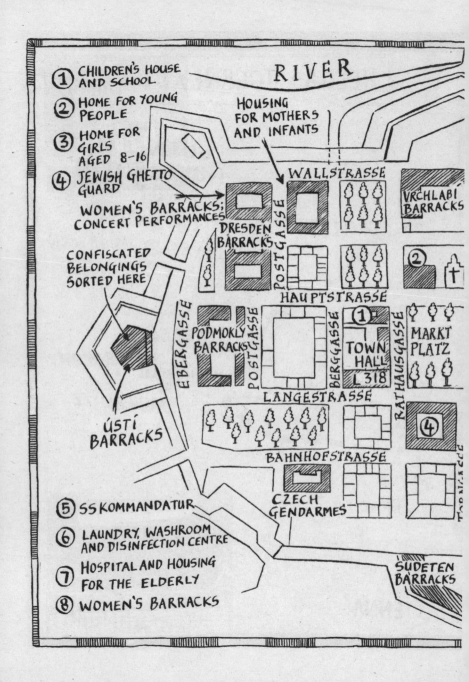

1. CHILDREN'S HOUSE AND SCHOOL
2. HOME FOR YOUNG PEOPLE
3. HOME FOR GIRLS AGED 8-16
4. JEWISH GHETTO GUARD

WOMEN'S BARRACKS; CONCERT PERFORMANCES

CONFISCATED BELONGINGS SORTED HERE

ÚSTÍ BARRACKS

HOUSING FOR MOTHERS AND INFANTS

RIVER

WALLSTRASSE

VRCHLABÍ BARRACKS

DRESDEN BARRACKS

POSTGASSE

HAUPTSTRASSE

EBERGASSE

PODMOKLY BARRACKS

POSTGASSE

BERGGASSE

① TOWN HALL L 318

RATHAUSGASSE

MARKT PLATZ

④

LANGESTRASSE

BAHNHOFSTRASSE

CZECH GENDARMES

SUDETEN BARRACKS

5. SS KOMMANDATUR
6. LAUNDRY, WASHROOM AND DISINFECTION CENTRE
7. HOSPITAL AND HOUSING FOR THE ELDERLY
8. WOMEN'S BARRACKS

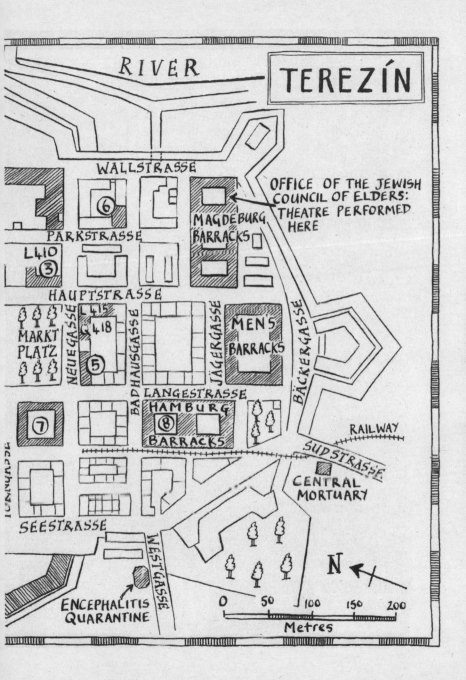

HELGA'S DIARY

Preface

With age, one returns increasingly to the past. To my surprise, I now find that I essentially never left it. After some years I read my diary again – carefully, from beginning to end – with a bit of nostalgia, I admit, and in many places with great emotion.

I don't really know how to start writing a preface to my diary, or why I should do so. Everything essential I recorded more than sixty years ago. I wrote down my experiences and thoughts, at first in school notebooks, then on individual sheets of paper. The writing is childish, the style prolix, naïve. Still, it is a faithful picture of the time in which my generation lived, grew up and died. Much has already been written, many things have been forgotten, occasionally matters have been deliberately suppressed and distorted. I like things tidy and don't want to leave a mess behind. It's high time I put my effects in order.

Over the years a large number of documents have accumulated. I don't enjoy sorting through papers and so mine are a bit chaotic. Thus I came upon my journal, put away years ago and almost forgotten at the bottom of a drawer. It's a stack of yellowed papers, written in pencil, in places hardly readable. I move with the times; I learned to use a computer and so page by page I typed it up and printed it out.

I found myself deleting things, shortening long sentences, omitting clauses, choosing more appropriate words and expressions.

Some might object that it needs professional editing. However, my experiences with this have not been good ones. Many articles, radio programmes and reports have already been written about my adventures. Editorial interventions have frequently changed the point of them completely, distorting or falsifying true events. I fear that, with changes, the authenticity and force of the narration would be lost. May readers treat this diary charitably and accept it for what it is.

My diary begins in Prague in 1938; it describes the occupation of Czechoslovakia and the conditions there – primarily the anti-Jewish directives in the Protectorate and life in the ghetto at Terezín. Before our deportation from Terezín to Auschwitz (September–October 1944), I gave the diary to my uncle Josef Polák, who took it and my drawings and bricked them into the wall of a building, thus preserving them. Shortly after the war (1945–6) I finished off my Terezín diary and wrote down everything I had experienced in the other concentration camps (Auschwitz, Freiberg, Mauthausen), where there had been absolutely no opportunity to write.

I recorded these events as they occurred to me in my memories, writing spontaneously, quickly, under the pressure of the experiences that filled me. I wrote on unbound sheets of paper, without even numbering the pages. It did not occur to me to check the dates – in many cases I hadn't even noted them down – and anyway at the time historians were only just starting work on their studies. Scholarly publications did not come out until much later, after I had finished my diary.

When I was preparing my diary for publication in book form, it was not easy to put the events in chronological order. If I have not been successful, may my readers be tolerant of this. I am not a historian and my diary is not a work of scholarship. My prior-

[4]

ity, the most fundamental thing for me, was the events and experiences, and these I remember quite precisely to this day.

Reliable facts can be found in the scholarly literature. From history textbooks, students can learn that during the Second World War six million Jews perished. The precise figures have been tallied and preserved in databases. All you need to do is click on your computer; the dates and numbers will appear.

Each number, however, contains one human fate, one story. My diary is only one of these.

I finished my notes with our May 1945 return to Prague and the words 'finally home'. However, there was no home to return to. My mother and I had nowhere to go; my father never returned and our former flat had been occupied. I was fifteen and a half and most of all needed to make up my missed school years. We began a new life.

Helga Weiss
Prague, 2012

1. Prague

What do they mean by 'mobilization'? All young men have to
join up. Why? Not long ago it was all about Austria, and now
it's mobilization again. People can't talk about anything else.
But what is it? Why aren't Mum and Dad home today? Instead
of telling me what this mobilization's about, they've gone to
listen to the radio. Anyway, it's just an excuse, because they
could listen to the radio at home. They must have gone to their
friends' house so they could talk about the mobilization. What
must they think of me? That I'm still just a little girl, with whom
they can't talk about anything? I'm a big girl already, I'll be nine
soon. My God, what time are the bells tolling? I have to go to
school tomorrow and I'm still not asleep. This silly mobilization
has made me forget about school completely.

What air raid? Into the cellar – now, at night? Why are you
getting me up, Mummy? What's wrong, what's happening? What
are you doing; you can't put my clothes on over my pyjamas . . .

The gong just sounded in the hallway, summoning us to the
shelter. Dad was pacing impatiently in the vestibule and Mum just
barely managed to pull my gym clothes on before we fled down to
the cellar. The porter opened the old storeroom, which was
supposed to serve as a shelter. There wasn't a lot of room; we were
packed together, but at least we all fit in. At first no one spoke, but
their fearful eyes asked: 'What will happen; what does it mean?'

However, in a little while the mood improved. The men tried to calm the women down, although they were just as upset themselves. They had more self-control and could crack jokes. About a half-hour later the blare of the sirens announced the end of the air raid. Everyone went back to their flats. The parents of my friend invited us to spend the rest of the night at their house. They sent Eva and me to sleep; our parents stayed in the other room, where they listened to the radio. Sleeping was out of the question. Why should we kids have to go to sleep when everyone else was up? And when we finally closed our eyes, the siren wailed again. It happened three more times that night and each time we went to the shelter.

We didn't sleep at all that night. We children couldn't wait till morning. We'd have so much to tell people tomorrow at school. Maybe there wouldn't even be school; that would be brilliant. The grown-ups had other things to worry about and so they weren't so happy when the siren went off. But fortunately everything turned out OK. They were just false alarms and there was no air raid.

*

In the morning, I went to school. The classes weren't much use. All of us were excited and tired from the previous night. We told each other our night-time adventures. There was stuff to talk about all day. After lunch (which wasn't much good; no one was in the right frame of mind to cook) the whole building met in the shelter again. This time it wasn't because of an air raid, but so that we could clean up the shelter, in case we had to spend another night in it. We threw out all the things that belonged in the rubbish; the women set to sweeping and scrubbing, while the men put together first-aid kits and made a secret exit. The mothers made bunks for us using the goods lockers. Finally, everyone brought a suitcase with supplies down. We spent a bit of time chatting and then everyone went home and waited anxiously to see what the night would bring. Against all expectations it passed peacefully. Despite that, Eva's father and mine decided that it was too dangerous to stay in Prague. That very afternoon they went to find a suitable flat outside Prague where we could stay until the danger was past. They rented us two rooms in a small detached house in the village of Úvaly. In the meantime our mums packed up and the next day we left.

When we saw that there was no danger threatening Prague, we returned home. In the meantime our president, Eduard Beneš, had resigned and Emil Hácha had taken his place. That was called the Second Republic. Then there was peace for a while, but not for long. One day our new president was called to Berlin, where there were going to be discussions about the future of Czechoslovakia. There was great excitement everywhere in the country. People felt nothing good would come of this. And they were not mistaken.

15 March 1939

In the morning, when I woke up, Mum and Dad were sitting by the radio, their heads hung low. At first I didn't know what had

[9]

happened, but soon I figured it out. A trembling voice came from the radio: 'This morning at 6.30 the German army crossed the Czechoslovak border.' I didn't really understand the meaning of those words, but I felt there was something terrible in them. The announcer said several more times: 'Stay calm and collected!' I remained in bed for a bit longer. Dad came and sat next to me on the bed. He was serious and I could see he was very upset. He didn't say a word. I took his hand; I could feel it trembling. It was quiet, broken only by the weak ticking of the clock. There was something heavy in the air. No one wanted to break the awkward silence. We stayed that way for several minutes. Then I got dressed and went to school. Mum went with me. Along the way we met familiar and unfamiliar faces. You could read the same things in everyone's eyes: fear, sadness and the question 'What will happen next?'

At school, the mood was sad. The happy chatter and carefree laughter of children had changed into frightened whispers. Clutches of girls deep in conversation could be seen in the hallways and the classrooms. After the bell rang, we went off to our classes. Not much teaching went on. We were all distracted and felt relieved once the bell rang again. After classes lots of our parents were waiting for us. My mum came for me. On the way home we saw loads of German cars and tanks. The weather was chilly; it was raining, snow fell, the wind howled. It was as if nature was protesting.

In this way we came under the 'protection' of the German Reich, without knowing how or what from. We also got a new name.

Instead of Czechoslovakia we are now called the Protectorate of Bohemia and Moravia.

Since 15 March there has not been a single calm day. There have been orders one after another that repress and wound us more and more. Not a day goes by without bringing some new turmoil. The worst of it has landed on us Jews. They heap everything on our backs. We're the cause of one thing after another, everything is our fault, even though we didn't do anything. We can't help being Jews, and nor can we help any of these other things. No one asks; they just feel they have to pour out their anger on someone and who's better for that than – of course – the Jews. Anti–Semitism is rising; the newspapers are full of anti-Jewish articles.

*

Anti-Jewish orders are on the rise. The news that Jews couldn't be employed in government jobs any more caused an uproar in Jewish families. Then, no Aryan (previously an unfamiliar word) could employ a non-Aryan Jew. Now they keep coming, time and time again, order after order. You barely know what you can and can't do. It is forbidden to visit cafés, cinemas, theatres, playgrounds, parks . . . there are so many things that I can't remember them all. Among others there was also an order that really upset me: the expulsion of Jewish children from state schools. When I found out, I was unhappy. After the holidays I was supposed to go into Year 5. I like school and the thought that I will never be able to sit at a school desk with the other students brings tears to my eyes. But I have to bear up; there are other things waiting for me and many of them will undoubtedly be much worse.

Signs in German and Czech at a children's park in Prague, 1939.
The uppermost sign reads 'Jews Not Allowed'.

1 September 1939

War has broken out. No one was surprised. The way events
turned out, we had to count on it. However horrid the prospect
that this could lead to a world war, it's the only hope – not only
for us, but for all enslaved peoples – to have a happier tomorrow.

*

Before I got back from the holidays, Dad signed me up for a group so I could keep up my studies. It's not like being in school, but I'm getting used to it and am starting to like this new way of learning. Our group is made up of five Jewish girls. Our teachers are two young students who had to give up their studies for the same reason we did. We take turns meeting in each other's flats. Instead of a school building like we were used to, it's an ordinary tenement; instead of a classroom, a child's bedroom. School desks are replaced by simple chairs and a table, the big school blackboard by a child's small slate.

28 October 1939

Another disruptive order. This time, for a change, it doesn't concern Jews, but university students. All the colleges will be closed down – because a few students tried to hold a protest. One of them was killed. At his funeral there was a repeat of the protest. But nothing was achieved except that a lot of students were dragged off to the concentration camps.

The arrests never stop. The German 'Gestapo' police rampage through Prague and arrest everyone it suits them to, as they say. Prague is full of these uniformed and plain-clothes Gestapo men. They spread terror wherever they go and everyone takes great care not to fall into their clutches. Despite people trying their hardest to stay clear, there are many unlucky ones who fall victim to their cleverly laid traps. Danger lurks at every step. When you leave your house, you never know if you will return. By now there are very few families who don't have one of their nearest and dearest in a concentration camp. Thank God we have been spared that so far.

⌒

Autumn 1940

Slowly we got used to the new regime. We grew numb. Even the sharpest decrees don't nettle us much. And there are a fair number of them.

All businesses have to be German-Czech. (Some enthusiasts take it too much to heart and only have German on their shop-fronts.) A notice was added to the menu in every restaurant, printed in bold letters so no one could miss it: 'Jews not allowed – *Juden nicht zugänglich*'. This sign appeared at the entrance to all entertainment establishments, sweet shops and barbers. Contact with Jews is being curtailed.

Despite this my Aryan friends have not stopped visiting me. They always bring their school notebooks, which Dad uses as a guide, because since Christmas he's been teaching me himself.

So I muddled through a whole year that way. I passed my exam at the Jewish school and got my report. All A's. Why don't I feel satisfied the way I used to? The marks still make me happy, but the knowledge that I'll be spending the forthcoming holidays in Prague fills me with sadness.

Last year, even though it wasn't as nice as the previous year, at least we were in the countryside. In a small town – more like a village – called Cerhenice. Dad was employed there on a farm, by the farmer. He went voluntarily, like many others, so he wouldn't be called up for other manual work. Staying there certainly wasn't ideal, but since there weren't many summer flats Jews were allowed to rent, I was happy enough with it. It was a long way to the woods and I only went swimming a couple of times at the beginning before the ban came in: 'Jews are forbidden to swim in the river' – just in case, God forbid, they pollute the water before the Aryans can bathe in it. But the relatives we were staying with had a big garden and a pool in it – a small one, but a pool nonetheless. Four of my distant cousins lived in the village and our other relatives had two daughters themselves. So there were seven of us and that was enough for us to play to our hearts' content.

We had a good time that summer and still I wasn't satisfied. It hadn't been like other holidays. What I wouldn't give now to be able even to go there! But that's not possible. Jews are not permitted to go more than 30 kilometres from their place of residence. Prague in summertime, dusty streets, ugh! It will be the first holidays I've ever spent in Prague.

These thoughts whirl around my head; it's why my school report hasn't brought me any joy. But so what: there are kids who have never ever been to the countryside. Why shouldn't I try it for once? After all, it is only once. Next year the holidays will be better. Of course they will; after all, this won't last forever.

⟨⟩

Summer 1941

And the holidays are here. All the Aryan children have left. The only one of my friends who has stayed is Eva – but not the Eva from our building, she's not my friend any more, not for a long time now. Since Hitler came she looks down on me; she probably thinks she's better than me. If it makes her happy, I'm not going to spoil it for her.

So only Eva stayed. We spend all day together. Eva's building has a small garden where we play. The shady area takes the place of a forest; the tub filled with water stands in for a river. We play for days on end and we're very good friends. Our parents have also grown close. On Sunday, when the weather is good, we take short trips together. When it's nasty out we visit each other. We come over soon after lunch and stay together till late in the evening. That is, until a quarter to eight, because after eight we are not allowed outside. We never want to go home and always look forward to the next day when we'll meet again. So day after day passes, the evenings grow shorter, the air grows cooler. The holidays are nearing an end.

◦━

It went by so fast. It wasn't all that bad in Prague; I had imagined it being much worse. The kids are returning from their holidays; school will be starting soon. I can't wait. I'll be going to the group again. I'm curious about our new teacher, our studies and my classmates. Why does time drag so? I'm counting the days till the new school year.

◦━

31 August 1941

Finally: school starts tomorrow. For a long time I can't fall asleep; I'm thinking. How will I like the group; will the classes be difficult? What will my fellow students be like? Will there be any boys among them? Lots of questions and no answers. I toss in my bed and can't sleep. I hear the clock strike eleven. I still can't sleep. Now I'm afraid I won't be well rested tomorrow. I try to force myself to drift off. I count to a hundred but it doesn't help. One more time, and again, I'm falling asleep . . .

My sleep is restless; I toss and turn and have strange dreams. In the morning, I'm the first one up; I'm afraid of being late and can't stay in bed. There's still plenty of time till we have to go and I'm already ready. I hurry Dad, who is supposed to be accompanying me. Why is he moving so slowly? He's taking his time with everything and I'm going to be late!

Finally he's ready and we set off. We're taking the tram. It's not far, only three stops. My God, everything's dragging today. The tram moves slowly; I wish we were there already. Time to get off! I jump down from the tram, from the back carriage – where else, of course, surely not the front one? That's only for Aryans.

We enter the building whose number we were given and stop at a door on the second floor. My heart is beating rapidly when Dad's hand touches the bell. I feel like a little girl going to school for the first time. The door opens slowly and there is a young woman standing there, my teacher-to-be. I look her over with a searching gaze. After a short conversation with her, Dad goes away, leaving me here alone. The teacher takes me into her room, our classroom. There is a long table and ten chairs. So we'll be ten, I suppose. I thought I'd be first but there's one boy here already, my future classmate.

I sit down on one of the chairs and look around at the room. Time is dragging again. I exchange several glances with the boy, but we've not yet spoken to each other. And now the doors open again and three boys come in. And then one more and another two. My goodness, is it going to be all boys? They all know each other; all of them came here last year. They have lots to talk about and they barely notice me.

I look them over curiously. I don't know any of them. Or do I? This, if I'm not wrong, is Honza. We knew each other years ago, when we were in Year 1 together, and over there, that must be Jirka. We took the exam together. A little while later a girl comes in. I relax – my fears were groundless. I quickly start a conversation with her. One more boy comes in. It's nine o'clock and the lesson starts.

During the break we introduce ourselves. I already feel at home. I know what each of their names is; I have to go over and over them so as not to forget. The one sitting next to me is Petr, then Jirka and then that one – what's he called? Aha, that's Pavel, and then another Jirka and Honza. Then after that is a second Pavel, next to him Luki and his neighbour, the little kid, has a strange name: Aristides. We call him Ari. Then there's Rutka and I. That's our whole group. I'll have to repeat it a few more times – maybe that'll help me remember.

After the break we had one more lesson and then we broke up with a cheerful 'See you tomorrow'. I hurried home, where Mum was waiting; she was curious how I liked the group. After lunch I'll go over to Eva's – she was at her group for the first time today, so we'll have a lot to talk about. At three – the time Jews are allowed to shop – we'll buy some school supplies. I'm looking forward to tomorrow.

5 October 1941

A month has passed. I'm completely at home in my group. Otherwise nothing has changed. In the morning I go off to school and return at noon, even though we finish at eleven. That's because the whole group goes to the playground – the Jewish one, of course. Meanwhile, Dad is at home, cooking. It might sound a bit strange, but almost all the Jews do that. What else should they do all day? After all, it's three years since they lost their jobs. It's wonderful what progress you can make in three years. Before, Dad couldn't even make tea, and now he bakes desserts and cooks entire lunches all by himself. He and Eva's dad compete to see who can clean up quicker and they visit each other to see whose floors gleam more brightly and who has the most sparkling stove or dishes.

After lunch, when I have finished all my homework, I go for a walk with Eva. Usually to the Jewish playground. We're both learning English from my father. I'm getting on well with it and I enjoy each new word that I learn. It feels like we could survive another few years of this life. But unfortunately the Germans think we are too well off and are now thinking of more things to spice up our peaceful life. This time they came up with a great idea that even the Middle Ages would have been proud of. Conspicuously labelling the Jews. Stars! Bright yellow, with the word *JUDE*.

It's almost a quarter to nine. Quickly, coat on, swift glance in the mirror to see how the new, bright yellow star sticks out, and now it's high time to get off to school. Dad's waiting; who knows how the Aryans will behave once they've seen us marked in this way. That's why, unusually, he's going with me today. The first person we meet is our building's caretaker. Why is he staring at us that way? But of course: he has to see how our new badges suit us.

On the street we meet with various sorts of glances. One person will pass by not noticing, at least apparently (no one can resist peeking just a bit); another will smile sympathetically or encouragingly; with a third, a mocking and sneering jeer will cross his mouth. Sometimes we have to put up with comments, but we're used to that already. We get into the tram, into the last carriage. Here things look a bit different: one star after another. And once we get closer to the city centre it's positively swarming with stars. We've reached our stop. I reassure Dad that he doesn't have to come and pick me up. I'm not afraid to come home alone; I can see nothing will happen. The reaction hasn't been as strong as the Germans imagined.

At school we all boast about whose star is sewn on best. Even though it's not pleasant to have to wear it, we make light of it. We've got used to other things; we'll get used to this.

In fact, nothing did happen and I got home safely.

In the afternoon, I go for a walk with Eva. Not to the playground today – we deliberately stay on the busy streets. It amuses us when we meet other Jews. They always smile, as if to say: 'Looks good on us, doesn't it?' We count how many stars we meet and compete to see who can count more. We talk gaily and laugh loudly. Let the Germans see that we're not bothered. We deliberately put on cheerful faces and make ourselves laugh. Deliberately, to make them angry.

*

Jewish schoolchildren in Prague wearing the yellow star.

A further month passed. The stars became something we took for granted, as if we'd been wearing them forever. But another new thing is coming to disrupt Jewish families. It's horrible; there's never been anything like it here before. No one knows anything definite, people just sense it. Supposedly there will be *transports*. Let's hope it's not true. No, it certainly won't be true, it mustn't! All it takes is someone to think it up and the news spreads like wildfire. Still, everyone would rather be prepared. We can't know what will happen and it's better to be ready and not go anywhere than to get the transport unexpectedly. And so Jewish flats are turning slowly, or actually quite quickly, into warehouses of things needed for the journey.

All the Jewish flats have been turned upside down, and ours is no exception. Everywhere – on the tables, the chairs and the ground – are stacked suitcases, rucksacks, haversacks, sleeping bags, warm underwear, sturdy shoes, flasks, mess tins, torches, pocket first-aid kits, canteens, solid alcohol, candles. If I wanted to write it all out, even the whole notebook wouldn't be enough.

*

Everyone is getting ready for travel.

The news about the transports wasn't made up and the preparations weren't in vain.

⸙

12 October 1941

So it's a fact now. 'They're sending out the announcements tonight' – everywhere you can hear the Jews talking about it.

Last night several hundred Jewish families got summonses for transport. Poor things, they couldn't even prepare properly; it was Saturday night. The day after, the shops would be closed and on Monday they'll have to go. If only we knew where it was going.

There is talk of Poland, but who really knows.

In all the excitement over one thing you lose track of another. We pack feverishly, bake, and at the last moment there are goodbyes. Thank God, this time there was no one from our family in it, only a few acquaintances. But what will come next?

No sooner had the first ones set foot in the 'Trade Fair' than there is talk of a second transport. Only now does the real packing begin. In all of Prague there is not a single proper suitcase, backpack or mess tin to be had. Every time you go past a Jewish flat there is the smell of fresh-baked goods. People are baking crackers, biscuits, Christmas cake. Everyone is getting ready for travel.

~

15 October 1941

I sit in the tram on my way to lessons. Last night there were more summonses. Again, my whole family and Eva's were lucky enough to escape. Now we'll see what happens at school. The woman sitting next to me, poor thing: she's crying. Someone close to her must be in it.

I've arrived; I'm afraid to enter the building. Which of us will be in it? And suddenly I can't stand it any longer; I want to know as soon as possible. I run upstairs and fly right into the flat. I stop, hesitate, open the classroom door with a trembling hand. I look around with an enquiring glance. I don't even have to form the question. 'Luki's in it,' I hear a choked voice say. I take my seat quietly. So Luki's in it.

Today our good mood falters, somehow. The doors open and Luki appears. We want to drive away his sad thoughts and make his last hours among us pleasant. We try to be as cheerful as usual, but the jokes just don't come. Luki's smile, too, is fixed. During the break we make plans; each of us is ready to bring something from what we've purchased to make up for what Luki still lacks. And they'll need a lot; after all, they've had so little time to prepare. Luki modestly refuses our help, but soon we convince him. Fine friends we'd be not to help him in such a situation.

That afternoon the whole group goes to the playground. All

[23]

together, for the last time. Tomorrow we'll be one poorer. We try not to let it show, so Luki can forget about it a little, although not entirely. The thought keeps coming back to us and we can't shake the mood. The smiles always die on our lips.

It slowly gets dark; the time for goodbyes has come. I'd like to go home already, but I can't bring myself to say it; I can't get the words out. And when finally that fateful 'farewell' passes my lips, I have to add quickly: 'I mean, goodbye, I'll be right back.' And so three times, I come back. Every time I'm about to leave, I have to turn round. After all, it's the last evening we'll be together. The last. We'll never see each other again. Until maybe 'some day'. It's childish to believe in it, but we have no other comfort.

At last it's completely dark. Now there's nothing for it, I have to just say: 'So farewell, then, Luki.' How meagre it is compared to what I'd like to say, but I can't force myself to say anything more. I feel my throat seize up and that one, meagre sentence comes out in such a strange voice that it frightens even me. 'Farewell', comes his quiet answer.

*

There were more summonses. Once again nothing. Now as long as Eva isn't in it . . . I stop at her house before going to school. I don't even have a proper breakfast; I just run to the Vohryzeks'. For a long time I stand at the door and am afraid to ring the bell. Until I do, I can always hope, but once I ring – no, I can't imagine it. I don't have the courage to ring. Through the door I can hear worried voices. Eva's at the door now. I hear three words: 'We're in it.' Only three words. I can't come up with even one. I have to go and get Mum so she can help pack.

At home I pour out, flustered, what I heard and then hurry

off to school, it's high time. Now all we need is for someone from the group to be in it. I arrive all out of breath. This time no one's in it; they were only afraid it was me since I took so long getting there. In the lessons I'm distracted; the teacher hears about Eva and doesn't call on me. At the break I don't talk to anyone. I keep thinking about Eva. If only lessons were over so I could go to see her. One more hour. I get nothing from the lessons. Half an hour more, a quarter, finally it's half past eleven, lessons are over.

From school I took the tram, grabbed some food at home and hurried over to the Vohryzeks'. The place has been turned upside down. Luggage thrown everywhere, clothing, food, agitated people. There's plenty of work for everyone. Numbers get written on suitcases, sewn on backpacks, haversacks, bedrolls. Underwear and clothes are sorted: what to put on, what to put in the rucksack – because what you have on, you can count on; only the less necessary items will go in a suitcase. Who knows whether they'll be delivered. They send Eva and me out, we're just getting in the way.

We go over to our place. We try to play as usual, but it doesn't work. The realization keeps coming back to us that these are the last hours we will spend together. We don't even talk much. Around eight I walk Eva home and come back with my parents. After dinner I go straight to bed. My head aches and I'm on the verge of tears. While I was with Eva I managed to suppress it, but now, alone, I feel fully conscious of it for the first time. I don't fall asleep till late that night.

*

Today again I get nothing from the lessons. I'm poorly prepared and my homework is full of mistakes. When I am called on, I don't know what I'm supposed to be answering.

That afternoon Eva is at our place again. We finish sewing outfits for our dolls. When we're done, we go to the Vs' to pack the toys. It's so difficult to choose the ones we love most. Eva has a whole cabinet full of them; she'd like to take them all with her. However, there are more important things to have with you on the road. For toys, the only room left is a small handbag. Finally Eva manages to speak and admits that since she's losing everything she owns, she will have to give up her toys as well. We chose a couple of her most beloved things. There are so few of them compared to the heaps of toys that are staying. And still they barely fit in the handbag.

Working together and eliminating a few more small items, we finally fit them all into the bag. On top goes the bag with the outfits we finally finished. Eva will carry the dolls themselves in the pocket of her coat, in their own sleeping bags and clothing with transport numbers. What if the handbag were to get lost? Then at least the dolls would be saved. Tomorrow is Sunday; Eva will spend the whole day and night with us.

There's been lots of progress with the packing, but there's still plenty to do. We keep coming up with new ideas for taking as many things as possible, for hiding contraband so they won't find it during the searches.

*

The three-day period has passed; tomorrow they have to leave. This evening the whole family is over at the Vohryzeks'. Together one last time. Will we ever meet again? Maybe, but it's more likely that we will follow them than that they will return. No, that can't be, some day we'll meet again in a well-heated flat and we'll remember things and talk about our sad, long-gone exile.

It might be a long way off, but some day it will happen and we will survive. We won't give in!

⌒

28 October 1941

5 o'clock in the morning. It's time to get up. The Vohryzeks report at six.

I don't even know how I got to the Vohryzeks' house. For the last time, I enter that friendly flat where Eva and I spent so many happy hours together.

The Vohryzeks are ready and just waiting for us. Their packed luggage lies ready on the floor of the entrance hall. On every piece, and on the coats of each member of the family, are pinned their transport numbers: 248, 249, 250. So they're no longer people, just numbers. A last scan through the flat to see if anything's been forgotten and then we are leaving the flat for the last time.

Eva and I go first. We don't speak. It's not necessary. We both have the same thought, and even if we wanted to, our choked-up throats won't let out a single sound. I try with all my might to stop from crying, so as not to make this difficult farewell even harder for Eva. Eva is also fighting her tears, but at the building gate she can't hold them back any longer. I want to comfort her, but my attempt at a consoling word ends up as a quiet sob. Now we can't stop crying. We walk silently side by side, holding hands, and the early-morning greyness is broken only by the occasional sobbing.

In this way we arrive at the stop, our parents following behind. They feel uncomfortable as well.

The tram carriage we board is completely empty. It is barely a quarter to 6. There are a few labourers on their way to work. The closer we get to Prague, the more the car fills up with members of the transport. The tram we transfer to several stops from the Trade Fair is completely packed. We have to wait on the platform. 'Trade Fair Palace!' the conductor announces. The carriage empties out. This is where our journey has led us.

Alongside the Trade Fair is a sprawling queue, which we too now join. The queue moves slowly, and yet we wish it wouldn't move at all. With every movement we're closer to the moment when we have to say farewell. The waiting is endless and still the moment of leave-taking grows irrevocably closer.

We're quite close to the entrance now. We can't go any further together. We have to say goodbye. But instead of words a torrent of tears pours forth. Now even our parents don't have the strength to hold back. The last kiss, the last handshake, and the marshals are coming to tear us apart. 'No goodbyes: anyone not on the transport has no business here!' One final glance, a wave of the hands and the Vs are lost among the mass of bodies.

And so I lost my last friend. Now I only see Rutka, Doda and sometimes the boys from the group. But none of them is as close to me as Eva. I think of her always. I will never forget her.

⌒

1 November 1941

Two further transports have left, but thank God we made it through, luckily. I have only one wish now. To celebrate my birthday, which is ten days from now, at home. Eva and I were so looking forward to it and now I'll be alone. I'll be sad. Last year a few of my Aryan friends came, but this year I wouldn't even dare invite them. They wouldn't come anyway; I couldn't ask it of them, it's too risky.

∾

The days go quickly by and 14 quiet days have passed since my 12th birthday. But today we got a fright. Mum and I were coming back from shopping and we saw an unfamiliar man with a star and a briefcase in his hand going into our building. By the signs of it, from the Council. There are no other Jews in the building besides us. What if he's bringing us transport orders? The thought flashed through our heads and we hurried quickly up the steps. The man was in fact about to ring our bell. We breathed easier – it was 'only' registration. Tomorrow at 1 o'clock we have to appear in Střešovice.

*

Registration is behind us now and we're just waiting to see when they bring the summons to transport. Though the news is circulating around Prague that the transports have been halted, no one believes it; it's too beautiful to be true.

But something has come true. Not completely, but at least in part. The transports supposedly won't go to Poland, but somewhere in the Protectorate. To a place called Terezín. It's an old military fortress, there would be plenty of room there for accommodation. We'll see whether there's anything to it.

*

We didn't have to wait long to see what came out of it. A few days after our registration there was a new summons. Once again we're not in it, but Uncle Pepa is. It's mostly men going; it's a work transport for the AK (*Aufbaukommando*).

⌒

4 December 1941

The clock has struck nine. Dad is reading the newspaper, I'm reading a book for fun, Mum has also sat down with a book – for the first time, now that she's finished sewing things for the transport. 'The transport could come any time now,' Dad says in a calm voice. Calm, because this isn't the first time we've waited this way. We've waited out several such evenings; will we get through this one as well?

Night-time quiet, interrupted by the sharp sound of the bell. Dad goes with an uncertain tread to the door. 'It's for you today, don't be afraid – after all, it's only *Terezín*!' says the man with the summons, trying to calm us down. 'Only': easy for him to say; he'd feel differently if the order was directed at him. Dad signs the summons with trembling fingers. After the man leaves we sit, motionless, for a while. I don't even realize that two huge tears are running down my cheeks. The moment I notice, I wipe them away. I won't cry! Dad and Mum aren't crying either. Mum has pulled herself together; she is hustling me off to bed and has already put the washing water on to heat up. Everything dirty will need to be washed overnight.

*

In the morning I wake up early. Still, both my parents are already
dressed. Did they sleep at all last night? I hurry to get dressed;
there's lots of work waiting for me. I have to let Grandma know,
while Dad goes to tell our aunts. If only they were in it too! We
could all go together.

We stand at the stop, waiting for the tram. As if on purpose,
none of them has a rear carriage. We've already decided we'll
have to walk. Finally one comes with a rear carriage. Dad gets
out first and I continue a couple of further stops on my own. At
Grandma's I'm slightly at a loss how to give her the news, but
she sees it in my face before I can open my mouth. I come home
with my aunt; she's helping us pack.

It looks awful here. Suitcases strewn everywhere, just like at
the Vohryzeks' recently. Aryan visitors come by every day; there
are lots of things to Aryanize. Each of them brings us something
for the journey.

*

The time has flown quickly; tomorrow is Thursday and we have
to go to sign up. Although a rumour is flying across Prague: 'The
transport's been halted, there won't be any more of them.' We
don't believe it.

Let's just have it; the delay won't last long in any case and
waiting like this without knowing is horrid. The only good thing
is that we can get packed in peace.

*

List of Possessions (7 January 1943)

Before being deported, the Jews had to hand in an inventory of all their property. This painting shows my mother counting the items of linen in the chest of drawers, while my father notes down the figures.

Today we found out that we have to board on Sunday. We'll have plenty to do to make sure we're ready with everything on time.

*

It's Saturday. Tomorrow we say goodbye to our home, our relatives and everything that was dear and close to us.

Our friends were here till late in the night. They came to say farewell. A sad evening – our last at home!

Tonight I'll sleep in my bed again, but tomorrow . . .? The visitors left long ago. I lie here and can't fall asleep. How long has it been since I couldn't sleep because of worrying about school. Barely three months. How silly it seems to me today. Back then I was afraid they'd not accept me in the group, and yet we all got used to each other. How hard today's goodbyes were. It's just a few hours since I said farewell to Jirka. He stayed till evening; he couldn't say goodbye.

After all, it was only yesterday that the whole group saw each other for the last time. Already it seems so long ago. And still I can hear their voices, feel the press of their hands. It's all gone now; I'll never see them again, never talk to them again. All I have left is a token from each one to remember them by.

I can't fall asleep and don't even want to. If I stay up, I'll prolong the night and put off the moment of departure . . .

7 December 1941

Five o'clock in the morning. The light is on in the living room; my parents are also up. My underclothes and dress are laid out on the chair. There are some notebooks on the desk; probably mine from school. On the doorframe opposite are hooks for the exercise rings. The piano stands in the corner. My eyes wander around the room from one object to another. Lying on my back, hands beneath my head, I etch all these familiar things into my memory so they will never disappear.

We sit down to breakfast – our last. Today everything, no matter what we do, is the last. Always the same thought: never again! My aunt and uncle arrive. We can go. I put on my coat; on it is my transport number, 520. And now it's irrevocable – we have to leave. Dad has locked the door of the flat and we go downstairs.

The building is quiet; all the inhabitants are still asleep. We go out on to the deserted street. Here and there the figure of a workman passes by, hurrying to work. Some give us a sympathetic glance; others pay no attention, or look at us with undisguised glee. Glee at our suffering, but by now we're used to such behaviour and no stupid smile or remark can bother us today. I notice nothing, automatically hurrying along so as not to be left behind. I can't manage a single word, sob, a single tear. Although I feel their pressure, I swallow their bitterness. As if in a dream, I walk, turning once to the windows of our flat vanishing in the distance, but my parents are already a way ahead and I have to run to catch up with them.

In the tram we meet several people we know who are going to the same place as us: the Trade Fair Palace. After half an hour, we get off. Not far away is that ragged queue; we join it – this time with the difference that we will not return from it. Instead, we'll go into the open gates of the Trade Fair, which will close behind us, and we will never again see our home.

But there's no time for such thoughts now. The queue in front of us grows ever shorter; the number of those waiting dwindles and the time grows closer when we too will have to enter those gates that await us so eagerly, open wide like a mouth lying in wait for its victims, so it can swallow us. The 'Ordners' – marshals – are here again, with their yellow armbands, to tear us away from our relatives. It has to be fast; there's still a long queue behind us. 'Hurry up, Auntie, one more kiss, don't cry – after all, you'll be coming soon too . . .' But the Ordners are impatient;

the goodbyes are lasting too long for them. We turn around a few more times, wave and then we're ripped away by the crowd, which carries us off.

All of this – farewells, leaving home and all these morning impressions – happened so quickly that we didn't even have time to absorb it. We stand at a massive table in front of a man checking us in. '518, 519, 520,' says Dad, announcing our arrival. We are sent to search out our allocated places.

The Trade Fair Palace is swarming with people. There are squares two metres in size painted in white on the floor. In each of them is a number and here and there are mounds of filthy, dusty mattresses. We finally get to the place marked with our transport numbers. We take two mattresses each from the mound lying nearest and sit down on them. We're tired, worn out and hungry. From our haversack we take out our snack prepared at home and start to eat. The Trade Fair is filling up. Everyone is on the lookout for his place, mattresses, luggage. I manage to find some kids I know who are in the same transport as us and, together with a few girls, we help distribute the luggage.

*

The Trade Fair is now full up. I return to my place. Some of our suitcases are already here and Mum is trying in vain to put together something that could pass for comfortable seating. We introduce ourselves to our neighbours, look around the Trade Fair and the courtyard and it's already 10.30; they are starting to give out lunch. We're called up by number; each person gets a coupon and we get in line with our mess tins. The hours pass quickly and it isn't even 12.30 when I approach the window in the kitchen – of course it's no luxurious kitchen, just a few cauldrons, an awning and a tub in which there is a cooked lunch. The cook puts a couple of potatoes into my mess tin, pours the so-called gravy over them and takes the ticket off me, so that, God forbid, I can't come back for seconds. We eat our lunch in the courtyard, where we then wash up our dishes at the spigot and go to have a rest for a bit.

I can't stay lying down for long and set off with a newly found friend to look round the whole building. Inside we soon grow weary: everywhere is nothing but dirt, dust, an unbearably heavy atmosphere, suitcases and between them people stretched out. We go out into the courtyard, past the kitchen, and get to two enclosures with the signs 'Damen und Herrenlatrinen'. The sharp stench of chlorine is enough for us and we don't even want to know how it looks inside. We meet a few other children and when we have had enough fresh air we go back to our parents.

Milk is being given out for children: more time waiting in the queue. After this snack I write a letter to Grandma. I add a little drawing of the Trade Fair to the envelope. With any luck the letter will get there – I hope so; there is a barber we know here who might deliver it for a cigarette or two.

*

The afternoon flowed past like water in a constant rearranging of suitcases, waiting in queues, the arrival of a few more 'Nachtrage' – latecomers – confusion and noise, interrupted only by a few 'Achtungs'.

After dinner we all stay in our places to prepare them for sleeping. But there's no thought of sleep. Our neighbours are talking loudly among themselves; a bit of humour is coming back.

We are interrupted from our lively conversation for the

hundredth time by a sharp growl, this time in a hoarse voice: '*Achtung, Achtung!*' An announcement follows that a German delegation is arriving. After this a deathly silence descends on the Trade Fair and shortly afterwards people in our area get up and stand at attention. I barely manage to jump up when several soldiers in heavy boots pass by us, looking severely around. After they leave I go with Mum to the '*Latrine*'. I've never seen one before and so I am curious how it looks inside. My curiosity, however, soon leaves me, for the moment I enter the gap in the fence under the sign '*Damenlatrine*' my stomach heaves in revulsion. Beyond the entrance is a narrow passageway: on one side is a wooden wall, on the other is the enclosure. Underneath an awning a board has been nailed and behind it a row of buckets has been placed. On them and around them chlorine has been spread. The ground is covered in puddles, or more accurately ice patches, because it is December and below freezing.

*

We get ready for bed. My day outfit is easily transformed into a night one: all I do is take off my shoes. Not exactly in the most comfortable position, but nonetheless I fall instantly asleep.

We are right next to the clinic and so we are woken every few minutes by the arrival of patients on stretchers. At first the sight of them makes me ill, but I soon get used to it. I will not let anything disturb me and I sleep without waking until morning.

*

It is barely six and everyone is already up. The noise here is like in the busiest of Prague streets. Everyone makes his 'bed' and then quickly rushes to the courtyard to wash. Mum and I go to the 'washroom'. Of course, this is no tiled bathroom with running water, but a rather ordinary shed with two benches and several nails in the wall. In the corner is a cauldron with hot water. It's not exactly ideal, but we're completely content, even ecstatic. What about the poor men? They have to wash in the courtyard. Brr, stripping half naked under the open sky and washing in icy water from the troughs, where your hands freeze to the taps.

After washing we go for breakfast. There is even white coffee – that's fantastic; it doesn't matter that it's not really white, more like grey, but at least there's some milk in it. It has no smell either, but so what? If nothing else, at least it's warm and the Christmas cake we can still treat ourselves to today will make up for its deficiencies.

'*Achtung!*' The whole Trade Fair shakes again with its sound. No one can leave his assigned place. We wait for the *Ordners* to come and they lead us away to a queue in the courtyard, and from there to an office where we deposit all our valuables. Money, jewellery, silver and the keys to our flats. Of course, only the things we took with us – there's no mention of the property already Aryanized. Understandably we declare a lot less than we have already hidden.

Our turn came around half nine and by lunchtime we were done. From queue to queue and the morning's already over. True, there's never a dull moment here. In the afternoon all the men had to go and have their heads shaved. Dad made use of the occasion to give the aforementioned barber his letter. He promised he'd deliver it; let's hope he does – after all, we gave him the cigarettes and the money we'd kept back that morning. It's certainly enough for such a small favour. We fill in a few more official papers and they're giving out children's milk again.

It's four o'clock. How time flies! It's almost two days since we left home.

I spend the rest of the afternoon playing with other kids; then dinner is given out. Soon after we go to bed. The noise at bedtime doesn't even bother me any more; I might not even be able to fall asleep without it. I'm woken up a few times by an *Ordner* who comes to shake Dad by the leg so he won't stop people from sleeping with his snoring.

*

Today wasn't at all interesting; everything was just like the preceding two days. Several queues, '*Achtung!*', a German visit, a walk in the courtyard, fill in a few more forms, and it's evening again. We don't cover ourselves with duvets today; they're already rolled up into '*Bettrolle*', so coats take their place. Our suitcases have been handed over; all we have on us is our '*Handgepäck*', because we're leaving tomorrow.

2. Terezín

5 a.m.

The alarm: time to get up! At six we start to board. We hurry to get washed – today just a little bit, only face and hands. We have to go and get coffee and fill our flasks with it, so we have something warm for the train. Shove everything packed into our rucksacks, put on shoes, get dressed and wait until they come for us.

'*Achtung, Achtung!* All numbers up to 50 board now; everyone else remain in your place.' The hours pass, we wait. '*Achtung!* Numbers up to 150, 200, 300, 500.' I am number 520. We're ready, waiting for the command. '*Achtung!* Numbers up to 550.' We go. They lead us to the courtyard; several hundred members of the transport are assembled here. We take up our assigned place.

Within an hour all thousand members of the transport are assembled in the courtyard. Several German soldiers stand with each group, their bayonets at the ready. Careful: everything goes quiet. A German officer (or something like that?) strides to the centre of the courtyard and prepares to give another speech. Deathly silence. A single booming voice sounds through the courtyard.

We receive some instructions regarding our journey, and afterwards we learn something that surprises all of us. That is, it would surprise us if it were true. Except we, unfortunately, are so used to these speeches and promises and have had several opportunities to see how true they are.

We are supposedly off to a new land to avoid persecution, so that we can start a new life. We will be taken care of, things will go well for us. We may be thankful that we are among the first and can help to build the ghetto and prepare it for the others who will soon follow us. This and other flattery come to our ears. It's just strange that none of this corresponds with the letters sent secretly from Terezín. We stare at the speaker and silently calculate how long we think he can keep speaking.

*

8 a.m.

The speech is over; the first 'crew' leaves for the station. We stare impatiently at the departing group. We're freezing; if only we could take our seats on the train. We shift from foot to foot, count the minutes. The hour hand is on its second time round and we're still standing in the same place.

We go out on to the street. In front of us and behind us are soldiers on bicycles. Pedestrians stop on the pavements and stare curiously at us. Tears even appear in some of their eyes; once in a while someone stands rooted to the spot with his mouth open as if he has seen a ghost. There must be something odd about us; the inhabitants of Prague don't get to see such a spectacle every day: people being led along the main streets in broad daylight under military guard, carrying all their possessions on their backs. Children, pensioners, doesn't matter, all with stars and transport numbers on their coats. It must be a spectacle, but it wouldn't stop the inhabitants of buildings near the Trade Fair in their tracks, because these days they must be presented with this view fairly often.

[41]

We take no notice of the curious looks; our thoughts are far ahead of us. After all, we don't even know where we'll sleep tonight, whether they'll tear families apart, what we'll have to eat tomorrow and other similar worries. We gaze at the streets of Prague for one last time. Who knows how long it will be before we see them again, if ever. A last walk through Prague. Many – no, certainly all of us – are crying silently, but we don't let our emotions show. What, and give the Germans the pleasure? Never! We all have the strength to control ourselves. Or should we be ashamed of how we look? Of the stars? Of the numbers? No, they're not our fault; that's for someone else to be ashamed of. The world is just a strange place.

The train station. They seat us in – or rather, load us into – one of the empty carriages. For now they're done with us. We take our seats, each in the place marked with his number. The luggage we put either above or beneath the seat. We can even remove our coats; the cold air warms up quickly with the breath of so many people. Outside it's a scramble; more groups are coming.

*

11 o'clock

All thousand travellers are in their places. So why aren't we leaving? The wagons are closed, each has its *Ordner*, armed soldiers stand on the steps.

Why aren't we moving? Perhaps so we can feast our eyes on Prague one last time? Thanks very much, what a lovely thought. What's the point in looking through closed windows? We're not allowed to open them. If only, for God's sake, we'd leave already; don't torture us with this waiting.

The train slowly starts to move. Are we really on our way? No, the train stops again, goes back to the station. More waiting. Everyone is sitting in their seats, many unwrap their sandwiches and start to eat.

Once more the wheels clatter beneath us, we think we're under way, but again the brakes screech. This is even worse than standing in one place. Could it be – finally – and again, no. And still nothing. Here, there, here, always in the same place.

*

Twelve

Two hours in the train. Again we leave the platform, pass the station, but we do not go back; instead, the train picks up speed. Everyone has gone quiet. Despite the fact that we had all wished to be gone, now that we're actually travelling an oppressive mood seizes us.

We will never see Prague again. Never! Why doesn't the train return once more? Once, just one more time. Let us say farewell to Prague for the last time. To our dear, beloved Prague, let us take our leave of her forever.

However, the train does not return, nor halt; it rushes mercilessly onwards without ever stopping . . .

Prague is far behind us. The factories and tenements have changed into small country houses, blackened streets have changed into meandering tracts of snow-covered fields. Prague is far away. The depressive mood lifts a bit.

We don't think so much about what has happened, but about what will come. More worries and pointless agonizing. None of us has ever been to Terezín before; no one knows anything –

[43]

just fuzzy, indefinite ideas. How does it look there; will our uncle meet us at the train station? A sharp opening of the doors interrupts my thoughts. Several SS men enter. '*Achtung!*' The word flies through the silenced compartment. Everyone stands to attention. '*Achtundzwanzig Frauen, sechs Kinder und sechsundzwanzig Männer*' – twenty-eight women, six children and twenty-six men – the pale *Ordner* reports with his heels together and arms at his sides. The SS man surveys him from top to bottom, casts a glance across the compartment and without a word leaves. We take our seats again. The conversation resumes its flow. A blow is heard from the next compartment. A woman by the door looks about to faint. It's the mother of our *Ordner*. Through a crack in the door she saw the SS man's heavy fist fall on her son's face. In his excitement he got his count wrong.

The woman has calmed down. The hobnailed boots in the next compartment have gone quiet. The *Ordner* comes back. He's fine, only his face is red and puffy, but he's laughing already. 'I won't die from a slap.'

*

Where are we now? That over there is Říp. I'd forgotten for a long time to look out of the window and meanwhile we'd travelled some distance. In a little while we'll be in Terezín.

The travellers are searching for their luggage, putting their coats on. Utter confusion everywhere. There's a scrum at the window. Outside are loads of men, each searching for people he knows. The train slows, there are several jolts and then it stops completely. The door of our compartment opens, letting us out. 'Anything you can't carry, leave in the train; you'll get everything.' We leave one bag and get off. Men in overalls, heavy boots, jumpers, riding breeches and caps. Lorries. The elderly and children can ride; the rest go on foot.

A bumpy road and a thaw. Our heavy feet sink into the mud and dirty yellow water squirts out from beneath the carriages laden with luggage. Behind each 'crew' there are carts in case anyone can't carry his luggage, and the men who push them readily answer our questions. We learn lots of unpleasant things. The worst – and we'd figured this would happen – is that men and women live separately.

*

Three o'clock

The first houses in the village. Curious faces look out of the windows at us; children run out in front of the houses to get a better glimpse. Why are there so few people on the street? After all, several transports have already arrived. I don't understand. What is over there, that big building? People are crowding at the windows, waving, but I can't make out any faces at this distance. Why are they all squeezed at the windows instead of going outside? 'That's Sudetenland, the men's barracks. They're not allowed out,' a man in overalls explains.

'Hello, Mr Hirsch,' a woman behind me calls. 'So, you too?' 'Yes, and how long have you been here?' 'I'm AK,' the man boasts. 'You've tried already, haven't you?' 'Don't even ask.' 'And how about your wife; is she at home?' 'Thank God, I was so worried she might come today.' 'Just be grateful for every day she's still at home. Even just the Trade Fair . . .' 'You're telling me . . .' I have no more time to take an interest in Mr Hirsch or even in the woman behind me.

[45]

In front of us is a large building – barracks, apparently. They lead us inside. 'Men to the left, women straight on.' But what's this – can't I hold my father's hand? 'Quickly, quickly, didn't you hear?' 'Farewell, Dad!' and then the current of people sweeps me along towards the courtyard. Arched windows one after the other, like a colonnade. Some people are already here, so we're not the first. All women, must be the women's barracks. Will we have to stand? I won't be able to hold out. Up since five, then the trip, I really can't, I'm terribly sleepy and tired. If only my feet didn't hurt.

'No, Mum, I'm fine, I'm just a little tired.' After all, I'm not going to tell Mum I can't hold out. How could she help? After all, she's no less tired than I am, poor thing. But it shouldn't have to go on this long. If only they'd take us somewhere, no matter where; if only I could sit down, even on the ground, just so I wouldn't have to stand any more.

*

Complete darkness, six o'clock. Is it possible we're finally on our way? Turn right, up the steps, keep going, one more flight. Along the hall to the left, turn the corner, into that room.

Number 215. Thank God, at least we're in a room. But where are we supposed to sit? There's just four bare walls. I really can't stay on my feet any longer. I sit down on the bedroll; next to me are Anita and another girl. Her name is Helena; we don't ask any more questions, we're too tired even to talk, our eyes are closing. If only I could sleep, lie down somewhere and sleep, that's the only thing I want right now. Just to sleep, sleep and forget about everything.

'Here you go, divide it up between yourselves.' Mattresses! I manage to get hold of one and now I couldn't care less, I can go to sleep. Goodnight.

Dad's luggage ready. From today he'll be living on his own, having to take care of himself. That will be something! Mum anxiously repacks Dad's suitcase, thinking of thousands of new problems, advising Dad what to do – there's no way he can remember all of it.

*

Half one

'Men embark!' We accompany Dad to the courtyard. For now we can be together. For now, but in a few minutes, maybe an hour or half an hour and then – farewell – and – maybe – no, I won't think about it. But thoughts go where they will. What comes next? Perhaps we'll never see each other again. 'Dad,' no, I won't, I can't speak. A whistle. We have to go. 'Helga, be good and if it turns out that . . . we can't know what will happen . . .' I bite my lip and hold back my sobs. I squeeze Dad's hand; it is hot and in his eyes – for the first time in my life – I see tears.

We feel – I can't find the word, and maybe none exists that could express the sorrow of this moment. And yet Mum and I will stay together, while Dad will be alone. It must be a hundred times worse for him.

Again the whistle, this time for real.

*

Half five

Hardly light enough to see and I'm still standing at the window. Around me everywhere are women with eyes red from crying,

[49]

fixed on a single point down there in the courtyard, where the heads of our loved ones are disappearing into the darkness.

It's so dark now that we can't make out the individuals. Everything has blended into a single surface blurred by our screen of tears. No one leaves the windows. With hungry, longing eyes, we stare at the last spot where we saw our husbands, fathers, brothers and sons. Even fourteen-year-old boys are counted as grown-ups and can't stay with their mothers.

13 December 1941

Three days in Terezín. We finally have all our luggage, we've tidied up our space – it doesn't exactly look pretty, but we've done what we can. There are 21 of us in quite a small room. Mum and I have 1.20 square metres. At night people lie in the middle as well and if anyone goes out they have to jump over them. We stick our feet in other people's faces – truly horrible. If you've not seen it with your own eyes, you would never believe it, and one day even we will find it difficult to believe that people could live in such conditions.

We've not seen Dad since Friday, but he sent us a letter through a man who has a pass. So one great worry of ours has been lifted: we know he's still in the same town as us. We can't have any contact with him, not even by writing – only when someone with a pass comes by and takes the letter with him. Of course a letter doesn't mean writing paper and a sealed envelope; it's just a scrap of skilfully rolled paper that can be hidden in shoes, stockings or elsewhere. They often have

The Dormitory in the Barracks (1942)

'There are 21 of us in quite a small room. Mum and I have 1.20 square metres. At night people lie in the middle as well and if anyone goes out they have to jump over them.'

pocket searches and God forbid if they should find a letter on someone.

*

A transport is supposed to arrive again today. I can't wait – maybe some of our relatives will be on it.

*

3 o'clock

I'm completely frozen. I've been waiting since 11 o'clock, and it must be coming any moment now. I can't let them slip by. Aunt Marta will be coming (my uncle spoke with her at the train station). I have to be here to welcome her.

∽

16 December 1941

Tomorrow we'll have been here a week. A week already, or just a week? A week is only a few days and yet everything – leaving home, the Trade Fair – seems like an eternity.

There was a men's brigade here the day before yesterday. Dad wasn't among them. Maybe he'll come next time. Actually I'm sort of glad he didn't come this time. It would have been worse than not seeing him at all. They brought the group of men into the courtyard of Dresden (that's the name of our barracks). They left them standing there for a while, wouldn't let anyone through to see them and then led them away. That was it. The women thronged at the windows just so they could catch a glimpse of their loved ones and send greetings with a gesture.

Yesterday another group came, still no Dad. For days Mum and I keep a lookout, so we won't miss him. Dad writes to us daily; he signed up to carry suitcases and they've promised him, supposedly, that they'll come here as well. Perhaps one day it will actually happen.

*

Today it finally worked out. They were bringing suitcases to Dresden. As usual, Mum and I waited in the gateway – more out of habit than any belief that he'd come. Suddenly a group of men with suitcases on their shoulders appeared, and Dad was among them. I was overjoyed – but made sure no one could see it. A kiss or something similar was out of the question, perish the thought – how could a man be allowed to meet with a woman, let alone speak to her? Even if it is his own wife. Here you're a prisoner and that's the end of it; such things don't happen here. But we understand each other even so, and we got lucky as well. The gendarme turned away. The men were not allowed to stay a moment longer once they'd dropped off the suitcases upstairs. We ran up to Dad, one on each side, and he didn't know who to listen to first. He didn't even get a word in edgeways, poor fellow. We had so much to say, but we had to say goodbye. We couldn't even show him where we're living. Let's hope he manages to come again soon. Perhaps he'll be able to stay longer. At the end of the stairs we said farewell. The gendarme 'coincidentally' turned around again.

Three days later Dad came again. This time it was with an official visit brigade. The men weren't allowed to go to our quarters, but we didn't bother asking. Dad just had a spot of tea and then we rushed back to the courtyard, so no one would find him in the room. We had a quarter-hour till departure time. We walked around the hallways for a while, but when we got back to the courtyard at half five, there was no one there.

Is the clock fast? Surely not. It's definitely half five; it's already dark. Could the others have left already? Gradually nervousness took hold of us. Maybe they're waiting in the other courtyard. It was already too dark to see properly. On top of everything it started to rain.

We were utterly desperate. We ran from place to place, turned our torches on, all for nothing – the courtyard was empty. What now? We stood helpless in the middle of the courtyard, so wet that the water was literally dripping off us, and not a living soul in sight who could advise or help us.

Should Dad stay overnight and worm his way into a brigade tomorrow? No point. At eight o'clock they check on us at *Standt*; by that time he absolutely has to be at home. There was nothing for it but to go to the gendarme and voluntarily announce the fact. But who knows if he's even on duty today. What if it's someone beastly who is on duty and he makes a stink over it? We were in a desperate situation.

At that moment the cooks rode by with a cart. A small spark of hope: maybe they can help or at least advise us. We were lucky. They hadn't been counted and so they could take Dad with them. How happily Dad grabbed the cart and helped push with all his might! The gendarme couldn't even suspect that Dad didn't belong among them. Let's hope that things go just as easily for Dad back at Magdeburg and no one will have the least inkling of our adventure. It's not even half seven; by the time they take attendance Dad will be long since home.

A View of the Barracks Courtyard (11 July 1943)

∽

If only Dad had come today. So many people we know are here, just not Dad – he's never pushy enough. Nothing left for it but to send the bread and sardines to him with someone. We had one tin left; Mum hid it away for today so at least we'd have fish for dinner. It's Christmas Eve. What a shame; it would have tasted better if we were all together.

We waited in vain until it got dark. We could have guessed that Dad wouldn't make it. He doesn't know how to work the system. Also, you have to grease a few palms, but Dad and greasy palms don't go together.

It's a crummy Christmas. I won't even see Dad and it's been

a fortnight since he was here. And on top of it they made caraway soup. Somehow the kitchen mixed up the menus. But what of it; we have it every day, so why not today as well? Because it's Christmas Eve? Stomachs don't know that and won't complain, and that's the main thing, after all.

In the room next door the girls prepared a show. Everyone from the rooms nearby came to see.

It was beautiful. We sang, the girls even acted out a short play. For a while we forgot completely. It was as if we were home, somewhere at the theatre, as if the candles set on suitcases and mugs were shining on a Christmas tree and we were at liberty and free.

No one is listening any more; no one notices the girls' songs and dances. They're not even dancing any more, actually. Their thoughts are somewhere else. They're no longer prisoners in these cold, dirty barracks. No longer do they face each new day with empty stomachs and constant fear. We're free, far beyond the ramparts and gates of the ghetto that hide so much suffering and woe, where death lurks for its thousands of victims – far from there, around a packed table, among so many dear faces and things – that's where everyone's thoughts are, and in the glow of the candles burning they see that beautiful, unforgettable image come alive before them . . . Home.

We were up long into the night, remembering our homes with tears in our eyes.

*

A week later we celebrated the New Year, 1942, in similar fashion, in the hope that it would be better than the last few. However, its beginning promised nothing pleasant.

I can't even write, my hand is trembling so much just from thinking about it. If I hadn't seen it with my own eyes, I would not have believed that today, in the 20th century, something like this could happen. This morning they ordered us to shut all the windows. We already suspected something. We knew that behind Ústí barracks they had put up a gallows. Around nine we saw (you can see through closed windows) a small group enter Ústí barracks. In the front and rear were the SS, in the middle nine young men with shovels on their shoulders – so they could dig their own graves! Nine condemned to death. What did these boys do that was so terrible to be dealt with so cruelly? Twenty-year-olds, maybe even younger, sent news about themselves to their mothers. So they sent the messages illegally? How else could they send them, when contact with home is forbidden? That's why they were executed. Why shouldn't it be possible? These days nothing is impossible.

I know they can be harsh and cruel, but today was the limit. They promised us we could go and visit our fathers on Sunday. All week we looked forward to it, couldn't wait, our fathers too; they'd put together a sort of concert, a festive welcome. My God, after all, it was to be the first time we'd been officially permitted to go on a visit. Our brigade was supposed to go at 2 o'clock.

Starting at 12, the courtyard was full of well-scrubbed and combed children in holiday clothes. After all, isn't it a holiday when we get to go and visit our fathers?

Then the order came to go back to our rooms. We wouldn't be going over to Magdeburg. A case of scarlet fever had been found among us; they didn't want us to spread the infection. We tried to protest, but of course to no effect. So we returned home with heads hung low, and this longed-for day ended in disappointment and tears. I got a letter from Dad in which he describes all the things they had planned for us and how they'd been looking forward to it. Perhaps they'll let us visit next Sunday.

Now I go every day with Pavel (an eleven-year-old boy from our room) to collect milk from the canisters in front of the commissary. A few times we had a row over it with some other children, but now we get there at half two. Then we're first and we have dibs on the milk. In the commissary they know us by now and sometimes they deliberately don't pour out the whole bucket, so there's up to ⅛ of a litre of milk left. Today we collected three-quarters of a litre all told. This morning we got hold of some turnips: one for Pavel and two for me. Yesterday they were putting them in the former mortuary for storage, but so what? Who would think about such things; hunger is unpleasant and turnip fills the stomach. Almost nothing is left of our stores from home and bread has to be hoarded. Our ration is a half-loaf for three days, and what's more it's mouldy.

Most of all we mustn't get caught. We crawled in through the window; it was easy, there was a cart standing beneath it from yesterday. Mum doesn't yet know; she's in Magdeburg with the '*Putzkolonne*', the cleaning brigade. She goes every day so she can talk to Dad. (I wanted to go too, but they wouldn't take me.) She'll be pleased when she gets back. I want to surprise her and get hold of some potatoes as well. You can collect them from the peelings in the room below in the passageway where they throw the kitchen rubbish. I've got the milk already; if I can acquire a couple of potatoes as well, Mum can make mashed potatoes. My mouth is watering already.

'Putzkolonne' *(Cleaning Brigade) (5 January 1943)*

Working in the cleaning brigade allowed one to visit other barracks. At a time when it was still not permitted to move freely in the town, before the original inhabitants had been evacuated, this was the only opportunity for men and women to meet or at least see one another from afar.

I'm uneasy about this transport. Dad said (this morning he managed to get over here again after three weeks) that it's stupid; where would it be going? But when people start talking about something, there's always some truth in it.

This afternoon, as I was coming back with the milk I'd collected, I found not a single person in the room. Where is everyone? I ran out into the corridor – not a peep. Where had everyone vanished to?

I made my way downstairs to the courtyard. What was happening? The courtyard was full of people and each of them was just pointing: 'Psst, quiet, there's going to be a roll-call . . .'

'Unfortunately, you were right,' Dad wrote to us. Yes, unfortunately, it was true. A transport of a thousand people will be going further east, they told us at roll-call. Everyone up to number 300 from our room will have to get ready. We're 500s, but who believes 'them'. 'I hope it all turns out all right,' Dad continued in his letter, 'but get packing just in case.' Well, that's nice. We thought at least now that we're in Terezín, we'd be spared any more of this. Now it seems to me that we'll never be finished with all this 'transporting', ever.

Last night the summons went out (thank God, we weren't included). This morning the transport boarded. Of course we didn't sleep all night. No one could know whether he'd be in it and so everyone packed just in case or helped those who already had the summons in hand. Many people we knew left.

Now in the barracks it's like after someone's died. The transport has left and the mood among those left has soured.

Prague has come. Three aunts and an uncle have arrived: Ola, Micka, and Frieda and Jindra. They're in the *Schleuse* in Hamburg barracks. We have to get to see them at any cost. It won't be easy, especially for me. They won't take me on any of the brigades, because I'm too small. I've not been away from the barracks since the time I went to Podmokly to gather potatoes. I've no hope of getting to the *Schleuse*, but at least Mum might. Frieda is in bed; she's got a high temperature – she fell ill at the Trade Fair. As long as it's not pneumonia. The doctor prescribed compresses. Who should put them on her? Jindra has already had to move out – people she doesn't even know? Here everyone's got enough worries of their own without taking care of anyone else. Mum has to get over there.

*

Frieda is in a bad way; Mum went to see her. They wouldn't take her to the infirmary; today they're supposed to be moving over here, to Dresden. There are some free places in our room since the others left. I hope we manage to get them all here.

*

We're all living together now. They brought Frieda on a stretcher; I've got to get a mattress allocated for her. Finally she'll be seen to.

*

No sooner was Frieda a bit better than Micka took to her bed.
Both had pneumonia. Mum had her hands full. She's not going
to work at all; for now they're not taking it too seriously. Now
Dad can get to see us more often; he doesn't have to lug suitcases
or shift potatoes. He got a place in the office and a pass, and so
it's always possible somehow to work it out so he can get an
official trip over to Dresden.

*

Micka was still in her bed and Frieda had barely got out of hers
when the news flew round again that another transport was to
leave. That morning Jindra wrote that he was very worried and
in the afternoon they brought Frieda the news. The office job
protects Dad a little, so we don't need to quake as much as the
others, but you can never know what will occur to 'them'.
Tomorrow a different order might come. No one here can be
sure.

*

There were a lot of people from our dormitory in this one:
another wakeful night.

*

The next day, the transport was supposed to board after lunch.
Frieda was all prepared to leave when they brought her the recall
notice. It took Dad and Pepa some doing to get her pulled out.

[62]

What's all this about Křivoklát again? It probably isn't even true, but anyway I don't have to go on the 'programme'. That's what we call studies, because school or anything like it is forbidden.

Our schooling moves around among the dormitories. Somewhere in a corner they free up a bit of space, everyone brings a chair (which our dads steal from somewhere – pardon, I should say they 'sluice' it, because there's a big difference – or they trade bread for wood, from which they bang together benches and shelves), a notebook and a pencil, and so we study. Sometimes we make too much noise and they throw us out of the room with our teacher. Other times a German visit comes through – someone always warns us in time, then we pack our things as quickly as we can and disperse.

So there's no programme again today. We have the whole day free. Except – is there any truth in the Křivoklát rumour? Supposedly a working transport of women is going to Křivoklát to do agricultural work. The summonses should be distributed this afternoon.

*

The transport has left. My aunts Ola, Micka and Marta have gone. I hope it's true that they will come back. They weren't even allowed to take all their luggage with them, only the barest necessities. That's not definitive, but it's generally said that it's just a working group and that they'll come back again. Let's hope.

We've moved over to the window, into the unoccupied places.

[63]

After all, it was time we moved away from the door. It's not as cold now as when we chipped ice off it, but given how freezing it was over there, I think we deserve a slightly better location. Dad still wants me to move out; they have set up special housing for children, the '*Kinderheims*'. Supposedly it'll be better for me there. I went to have a look; it is actually nice there, but I'd just rather live with Mum.

Our schooling is more regular now. Classes take place either in the loft or in the *Kinderheims*. Maybe I will move there after all. It's better to live with kids than among adults in the dormitory.

⌒

It's nice here in the *Kinderheim*, but I am really homesick. I know it's silly – after all, Mum is just one floor up – but I can't help it. It's fun here during the day, we're all the same age here, we study together and in our free time we play. We take turns doing '*Zimmertour*', cleaning up in the room; we call it '*Toranuth*'. We have dinner together round the table and then we make up the couches, always two and two; I'm together with Dita. Now we hear they're even going to put up bunks for us. In short, everything's better here than in the dormitory. If only I weren't homesick all the time. If it were up to me, I'd move back, but Dad won't let me. I suppose I'll get used to it.

⌒

What kind of Mother's Day is it when I don't even have a flower for my mum. But where to get it, when I can't get out of the barracks? I know; I'll make it out of paper – I've got crêpe paper in several colours. I'm sure I can manage it. But what else? A flower on its own, and not even a real one, isn't a proper present, after all.

I have an idea. The girls and I will make paper hearts together and Dad will write a message inside. This afternoon, kids get dessert rations; I'll hide mine and this evening, before Mum comes from work, I'll get it ready for her.

*

By some quirk I got lucky; I don't even know how it happened. In the kitchen they gave me an extra dessert. They're quite large slices of cake; I'll make the two into four and I'll have a present for Mum. I went to look in the *Schleuse* – some people we know have arrived and I got a few biscuits. I added them to the plate with the dessert and it looks really pretty.

It's not much, but after all, Mum knows there's not a lot of choice. Anyway, next year I'll make it up to her. By that time we'll surely be home! If only Dad could come see us as well – then it would really be a holiday.

*

Křivoklát has returned. So this time they were right. Everyone's gorgeously suntanned – especially compared to us, since we're still locked up in the barracks. They were in contact with some Aryans and brought back lots of stuff (eggs, cheeses – things we've not seen for the longest time) and, even better, good news. It'll all be over in two months, they say.

Now only the Vrbas are missing and we'll all be here. Grandma and Aunt Vally arrived yesterday. Hopefully they won't get shoved straight on to a transport. People are talking about transports again.

It's nice here now, as nice as it can be in this place. We got Grandma and Vally here in 217. Mum has a couch she shares with Frieda and Marta; Ola and Micka live in another room. I'm the only one who has to live apart. I'm desperate to move back in with Mum, but Dad won't hear of it. He says I should be glad I'm living in the *Kinderheim* and one day I might be glad when I think back on it.

Maybe he's right. Grown-ups have other worries. The transports are starting again. A commission is meeting at night; they've started to draw up the roster. We hear that they're mostly for the women from Křivoklát.

*

Two days have passed and I won't forget them soon. How could it be that they only put Ola in, and left Micka out? That's gratitude for you – after all that donkey work at Křivoklát. First they promised them the earth and then stuffed them all in a transport. But did we really expect anything better from them? It turned out well, we got Ola out. Other than that no one was in it.

1 July 1942

I must be sure to remember this date. The opening of the ghetto. We're allowed to walk freely in the streets. Only with a pass during the day, but at night everyone can. What a wonderful feeling it is to walk alone, without surveillance – where I want, like a free person. It must be a small step on the way to freedom; the end of the war must be near.

They got permission to build a playground on a huge field on the citadel ramparts. I go there every day. We're doing better for food; Mum has started sewing for people. You can't earn a lot, it's true – for a dress sewn completely by hand you get a loaf of bread – but even that means a lot to us. In general it's all much better than when we came. After all, back then there was absolutely nothing here, not even nails in the wall. We began to build like real pioneers, from the ground up, with bare hands. Today, half a year later, we've got a decent bit of work done. They started with building bunks; theatres are being set up in the lofts. I have been to a couple of shows already. Soon will be the premiere of *The Bartered Bride*. The houses the Aryans moved out of have been cleaned, the streets divided into blocks and signed, vertical ones with L and cross-streets with Q. The new transports get moved right into the blocks.

In the next few days we should start moving: all the working women into Hamburg, the office workers will go from Magdeburg to 'Sun' (the former hotel), mothers with infants to *Säuglingsheim*, the infants' home; children to *Kriechlingsheim* and *Kinderheim*, the toddlers' and children's homes; older girls to *Mädchenheim*, the girls' home; the boys to *Jugendheim* and *Lehrlingsheim*, the boys' home and apprentices' home. The officers, the so-called 'upper crust', got their own rooms in Magdeburg.

The L410 Dormitory (1943)

'They divided us into rooms by year of birth. So I was put in twenty-four. There are 33 of us here; we have triple-decker bunks.'

Our Dresden *Heim* has moved to the former German commander's house on the square by the church, to *Mädchenheim* L410. They divided us into rooms by year of birth. So I was put in twenty-four. There are 33 of us here; we have triple-decker bunks. During the day we study together and can only go out as a brigade. Mum is ill; she has a middle-ear infection and I can only go and see her for an hour each evening. I'm horribly homesick.

I live with one girl who's four days younger than me; her name is Francka. Our mums figured out that we were both born in the same maternity ward. From that day on we were friends. It's just interesting that we met this way. We should be sharing a bunk since we're friends, but Francka didn't want to leave her single bunk. In an unfortunate accident, however, she fell off it and her mum wouldn't let her go on sleeping on the third level. She was lucky that basically nothing happened to her. She cracked her head a bit, but only a little. It's not nice of me, but I'm just a bit glad it happened, because by coincidence there was a free spot next to me and so Francka moved over. Now I'm not as homesick – neither of us is, because Francka's just the same as me that way. In bed, we talk long into the night and have no time for crying. Anyway, why should we be weeping? We're all young girls, after all, we're supposed to be cheerful, no snivelling allowed. That's everyone's view and if we want to be on good terms with them (and we do), we can't go against that motto.

In any event there's no reason for crying. Maybe because we're imprisoned, because we can't go to the cinema, the theatre or even on walks like other children? Quite the opposite. That's exactly why we have to be cheerful. No one ever died for lack of a cinema or theatre. You can live in overcrowded hostels (there are relatively few of us here, only 33), on bunks with fleas and bedbugs. It's rather worse without food, but even a bit of hunger can be tolerated. 'Where there's a will, there's a way . . .', only you mustn't take everything so seriously and start sobbing. They want to destroy us, that's obvious, but we won't give in. We'll hold out these last few months.

I wouldn't move out of here now, even if I could. We have a fabulous group. We study Czech, geography, history and maths under the leadership of a *Betreuer*. We're thirteen, after all, and we've only finished primary school. What will happen to us after the war? We usually read in the evenings. Sometimes on our own, sometimes we read aloud to each other. There's a good choice of books here. That's understandable. When we packed our fifty kilos of luggage, there wasn't much room left for books; nonetheless, each of us took his most valued ones. Together we read Čapek's *First Team, R.U.R., The Mother* and Hugo's *Les Misérables*. We read the poems of Jan Neruda, Jiří Wolker; I know by heart 'The Ballad of the Stoker's Eyes', 'The Sailor', 'The Unborn Child'.

Yesterday I went to see *The Kiss*. It's playing in Magdeburg, up in the loft. Even though it's sung only to the accompaniment of a piano, with no curtains or costumes, the impression it makes couldn't be greater even in the National Theatre.

The Vrbas have arrived. Now, of all times, when a transport will be leaving and there aren't many people. My cousin has been here for a month already; the whole time he's been working on the *Bahnbau* and they promised him that this would protect his whole family from the transport, but as there are five of them, that will probably be difficult. It really doesn't look good with this transport in general. They don't even want to let them off the *Schleuse*.

Opera in the Loft (December 1943)

There were many artists and scientists in Terezín, and in spite of the inhumane conditions the cultural life was rich. Literary recitals, concerts, plays and lectures were held in the dormitories, lofts and courtyards. They were a source of hope and strength, and people, including children, took a great interest in them.

*

Dad, Pepa and Frieda did what they could, but there were too many of them. Pepa would have been able to stay – the *Bahnbau* protects him – but not his family. He didn't want to let them go alone; he went voluntarily. They left this morning. Straight from the *Schleuse*.

*

The Vrbas had hardly left when a new transport was announced. Grandma and Vally were in it. We couldn't get them out. Mum wanted to join voluntarily, and then Frieda did. In the end, though, they stayed.

⟡

Altertransports. 10,000 sick, lame, dying, everyone over 65.

It's horrendously hot. Sunbeams fall directly on my bunk; they reach further and further as I shrink from them in vain, withdrawing into the shade.

Today I'm not going to volunteer to help out with the *Hilfsdienst*. I've not missed a day so far, but I'm too exhausted to see all that misery and suffering. *Altertransports*. Young people aren't allowed to join them voluntarily. Children have to let their elderly parents leave and can't help them.

Why send defenceless people away? If they wanted to get rid of us young ones, that I would understand. They're probably afraid of us; they don't want more Jewish children born. But what danger are these people to them? They've already had to come here to Terezín; isn't that enough – can't they let them die here in peace? After all, that's what awaits them. Half of them already die in the *Schleuse* and the train.

The ghetto guards are shouting and running about beneath our windows; they're closing off the street. Another group's on its way. There's a stretcher, a two-wheeled cart with corpses, baggage and a *Leichenwagen*, a hearse. The street glazed with

[72]

August glare is shrouded in thick, filthy dust. Suitcases, stretchers, corpses. That's how it goes, all week long. Corpses on the two-wheeled carts and the living on the hearses. Everything here gets transported on these vehicles: dirty laundry, bread – we have one of them in our *Heim* standing in the courtyard. It has a sign on it: '*Jugendfürsorge*' – 'Child Welfare'.

What of it; a car's a car, no one's stopped to give it any thought – but for it to be carrying people, that's a bit much.

Again the rumble of carts beneath our windows. Two *Transportleiters* – the transport organizers – are walking; their cargo; and behind, several *Krankenträgers* – stretcher-bearers – and the *Hilfsdienst*.

Are those corpses among the suitcases? No, one of them is moving; through the screen of dust whipping around the vehicle a yellow armband shines. Who could forget them? We met them daily near the kitchen. On crutches, blind, with a little bowl in their hands, asking for a bit of coffee, soup, scraping out the unwashed tubs and basins used for cooking, or raking through the mounds of rotten potatoes, peelings and rubbish. Yes, it's them: emaciated, hungry, pitiful. They, the living on the funeral wagons. How many of them will make it there, how many will come back?

All the hearses are in use. For the first time, they carry a living load. And yet for these people nothing could be more appropriate. Where will these wrecks of human beings go; where will their bodies be thrown? No one will weep for them, no one will lament their passing. Until some day there will be a mention of them in our textbooks. Then the only fitting title will read: 'Buried Alive'.

Scraping out the Leftovers (10 March 1943)

Old people were the worst off as they received the smallest rations.

Three young lads escaped. For that, we've had *Kasernensperre* – curfew – and *Lichtsperre* – blackout – for a week already. We can only go to work in brigades; no one is allowed out on the street after six. We come back from work in the dark; in the morning we leave when it's still dark as well. We get dressed and undressed by memory. The windows have to be darkened and it is forbidden to shine any sort of light. Tomorrow I'll go to Hamburg barracks for bread; maybe I'll manage to pop in to see Mum.

*

Kasernensperre has been called off, but apparently *Lichtsperre* will remain all winter. We have to save electricity. It hits each block in turn every third day. We're allowed to light candles, but they don't last us long. Our reserves from home are running low and we won't be allocated any more. It's horribly silly; we can't even read in the evenings.

Without light, everything's sad and gloomy. I miss Prague horribly. Night after night Francka and I relive it endlessly; often we dream of it in our sleep.

Today I had a beautiful dream. I dreamed I was home; I saw our flat and our street absolutely clearly. Now I'm disappointed and in a bad mood, because I woke up in this bunk instead of in my own bed. Maybe, however, it's some sort of sign the end is near. But then there should be an eternal *Lichtsperre* across all of Germany.

It's incredible how time flies. In a couple of days we'll have been here a year. Last year I never thought I'd be spending my birthday here. And it was pretty nice. I got several cakes – of course, only Terezín ones – a charm – my transport number – and lots more things. We just got a package too. Packages have been permitted for about a month now.

With so few opportunities for amusement here, we seek out every possibility, such as one of our birthdays, to have a bit of refreshment, put on a play, etc. And because there are mixed-race girls with us in the *Heim*, we decided to celebrate both Chanukah and Christmas. We can't wait, and because Chanukah is before Christmas, the main preparations have gone into the first holiday. Each of us has to prepare 32 presents, one for each, or even more. Chanukah is in a fortnight. Starting today, none of us can eat sugar or margarine; our whole ration gets saved for cake. Anyone who has someone in the kitchen or gets a package puts their jam in. The day before the celebration we're not going to have dinner; we'll save all our potatoes for the meal together.

A potato gateau for the holidays? Here in Terezín we have fabulous recipes, of a sort not known elsewhere. For instance, bread cake with poor-man's cream; it's a delicacy.

*

We didn't have a Christmas celebration together, because the majority of the girls wanted to be with their parents. On New Year's Eve there was a masked ball; we were up until half one. All the *Heims* went visiting to wish people a happy new year. So many of them have disappointed us; will this one be better?

[76]

14 days after the New Year (1943)

'Girls, Vilík is on his way; he was just on the first floor. From number thirteen Dáša, Věra and Hanka are in it. He's in number twenty-five now. Dita, Eva, Danka and Líza.'

Vilík stands on the threshold of our door; all eyes hang on his lips. Who – am I in it as well? A couple of white paper slips tremble in Vilík's fingers. He looked slowly around the room and his eyes stopped at me. 'Helga, come sign this for me.' I'd never been out of bed so quickly and so quickly dressed.

It was late in the evening and we were all in bed already. Meanwhile, my aunt came and took me with her to Magdeburg. We waited in Dad's office until around midnight. They'd promised him; we wouldn't even have to pack.

I spent the rest of the night at Mum's and didn't return to the *Heim* until morning. The girls waited impatiently to see what my news would be and were tremendously glad that we'd had a promise. However, promises don't count for much, so just in case we set to packing.

The transport would board that evening and by eight we still had not had a recall notice. Dad got a confirmation, finally, so we didn't have to board and overnight they brought the recall notice.

This isn't a *Heim* any more; it's a regular hospital. Everyone avoids us; half of L410 is in bed. The thermometers won't drop

[77]

below forty. The number of sick rises every day; the infirmary can't cope. The rooms are full of sick people and the doctor doesn't know what to do.

I don't feel very well; I'll probably take to my bed as well. I've had every illness that's passed through here . . . 'Girls, whichever of you is going over to Hamburg, tell my mum I won't be coming today. My temperature's at 38.'

They took Zorka to the infirmary yesterday; she's in a bad way. The doctor doesn't have much hope. It'll probably be typhus. They want to quarantine us; they suspect all of us.

It looks awful here. No more than three of us in each room are well. Even Dáša, our *Betreuerin*, didn't come in today. She's been walking around with a 38-degree fever all week.

*

Yesterday they took Lilka's sister to Vrchlabí barracks; she's unconscious. They're setting up a new infirmary. Brr, I'm so cold again; I definitely have a fever . . .

*

Yesterday I had 40.3. My nose was bleeding. I was in horribly bad shape. They couldn't stop the bleeding; finally the doctor came. I thought I'd die, that's how ill I was. Today I feel a bit better; I just hope my temperature doesn't rise.

I was lucky; my temperature broke on the very day when everyone with a fever higher than 38 degrees had to move to the infirmary. It's typhus. I don't know – maybe I had it, maybe not. At any rate, my temperature wasn't up and they didn't send me to the infirmary.

There's an enormous sign on the doors of L410: '*Achtung* –

Infektionsgefahr'. Everyone's fleeing. Lilka's sister died and Lilka herself has typhus. Věra, Olina and Marta have gone to the infirmary. Yesterday they took Milča to Vrchlabí barracks; I hear she's in agony. Dáša and Zorka have died.

*

Typhus raged terribly across the whole of Terezín. The hospital and infirmaries were packed. They emptied out a whole house and made it into a typhus ward. Everywhere you can see signs: '*Achtung – Typhus*'; all the water pipes and pumps have '*Nie vergessen Hände waschen*' – Do Not Forget to Wash Your Hands. However, there's almost never any running water.

*

Shops are opening and we hear everyone will receive money for their work. What are we supposed to think about this? It's laughable, after all. Shops, money! What for, and for whom?

*

We thought it was strange that they were really going to start selling things here, but no one ever imagined they'd do it in this way. A whole transport simply had its luggage confiscated, and immediately there are goods for sale. There is a shop here with dishes, suitcases, clothing and sheets, a perfume shop and a grocery. Our pay is divided into four groups; special money is printed – *Ghettogeld*. We received points for everything. Every six weeks it's our turn for groceries. Mustard, caraway, celery salt and spread are available.

It does look like a real town here now, but I simply don't understand what they mean by doing this. If the rooms serving as shops were freed up for people to live in, it would definitely be more useful. On the one hand they're sending transports away from here, while on the other they're playing games like this.

*

And now another transport. We hear it won't go to Poland; the front's already there. It's for a new camp on the Polish border, somewhere near Bohumín. It's probably the same everywhere.

*

Things look a bit livelier here again. Girls are slowly returning from the hospital. Even Miluška will be getting out. We had very little hope for her. Even the doctors had their doubts; her life was hanging by a thread. Tomorrow Olina, Růža, Alena and Marta will come back. Thank God. It's the old twenty-four again.

We all signed up for work in the garden.

It's great there. We are working outside the ghetto and have a group pass. We all got into the same group. It's fun even just being out in the air. That's the difference between there and here. You can even see it in the way we look. We've been going there for barely a fortnight and we've all got red cheeks – and it hasn't even been that nice out; wait till the sun starts to shine! If only we didn't have to get up so early. And that endless hoeing – I can't wait till we're done and can start sowing.

I'm really looking forward to bringing Mum some vegetables. Maybe even today, if we go to Kréta to pick spinach. I have to get ready in any case, so I can 'sluice' some through. It'll work if I put on plus-fours, or should I put my gardening trousers on over them? Oh, Katka has a great idea. She unstitched the lining of her sleeve; it makes a wonderful pocket. It's a quarter past; in a little while we'll be forming up.

⌒

A lecture on Rembrandt was held in the boys' house, with lantern slides. It was very interesting. I hope they keep having these lectures; I'll definitely go again.

We all went to a cultural evening; they recited Villon's poems. It had a powerful effect on me. They're frightening and beautiful at the same time. 'I'm dying of thirst beside the fountain, / Hot as fire, and with chattering teeth: / In my own land, I'm in a far domain: / Near the flame, I shiver beyond belief'. I have to borrow these poems from somewhere.

Mum is moving again. Out of the blue some women from the *Landwirtschaft* – the agriculture department – came and of all places it was her room that took their fancy. Because it's the *Landwirtschaft* and in addition they probably have some pull in the *Raumwirtschaft*, our space management unit, they got the room allocated to them and the rest of the women had to move out within 24 hours. We've been here a year and a half, but what does that count for if we don't have any pull? Mum wasn't allocated to another room and so she has had to move to the loft.

⌒

Finally, after three months, Mum got a place in room 84, again with Frieda, on the third floor by the window. Pretty nice – most importantly it's not visible, so in the evenings when we all meet, we can climb up there and have supper in peace, without getting in anyone's way or anyone getting in ours.

⌒

September 1943

The girls are crowding at the *Waschraum* door; some have taken washbasins and laundry out to the courtyard. The benches, bunk ladders, everything that touches your hand stings. The stove can't heat all the water; the washing gets done cold. Between the puddles of water and the dirty laundry, on the bunks, the corridors, anywhere there's a bit of space, are piled suitcases, rucksacks and all our luggage. Nimble fingers mend everything that's torn. 'Girls, which of you will be finished first; I need to reserve a washtub. Where have you been, Eva, in Magdeburg? What's the news – how many, 1,500?!'

That afternoon the announcement came. Máša, our *Betreuerin*,

Renka, Gita and Ema. For now we're not in it, but they've still to announce the reserve list.

*

'Helga, get up, we're in the transport,' said Mum when she came to wake me early this morning. A little while later, Vily brought me the summons. We're way up in the reserves.

The reserve list is running the *Schleuse* in the brewery. It's 5 in the afternoon. I have to board. Vily is calling already. 'So, Máša, goodbye, I won't say farewell – after all, we'll see each other again soon and we'll found a new number 24 in Birkenau or wherever it's going. Franci, I'll hold a bunk for you next to me. Girls, come have a look in the *Schleuse*. Gita, Renka, are you ready? So once more, girls, farewell. Farewell, number twenty-four.'

*

Rather than be on the reserve list again I'd rather just leave straight away. How much luggage have we hauled? We kept not wanting to send our suitcases off, in case they sent them onward while we stayed here – and the fear of it happening the other way around. We could ignore all that – the fact that we didn't sleep all night and that we dragged our baggage at least twice from the loft down to the courtyard and back up again – if it weren't for the dreadful uncertainty. If only they'd just run it correctly, by the numbers, but *Transportleitung* – the transport administration – did whatever they felt like. In the end the highest reserve numbers went and the rest stayed here. I can't remember how many times we were assembled in the

[83]

Summons to Join the Transport *(24 February 1942)*

The summons to join a transport was delivered mostly at night. The location and the time to assemble were written on a slip of paper.

courtyard; I only know that at some point I just wanted to be on that train.

One time we were already on the way to the train. If not for Mum, we'd already be gone. On the way she turned around and saw there was no one behind us. We came back to the *Schleuse*, hid out for a while in the courtyard and then they let us in. Luckily we were among the first to get out of the *Schleuse*, because then suddenly they didn't have enough people and they were taking anyone they could find, even right off the street. Our girls – Gita also stayed – were waiting in front of the brewery and walked us back to the *Heim* in a festive parade. Francka made my bed up for me straight away and soon after that I fell asleep. I've never slept so well in my bunk. Now I want nothing more than to wait out the end of the war in it.

⌒

The buildings near the Sokol hall have to be cleared out. A special dinner is being cooked; we're preparing an *Entwesung*, a disinfestation. Some Polish children are supposedly coming. It's all so incomprehensible. Why and for what purpose are they bringing them here from Poland?

They arrived yesterday at 5 p.m. No one is allowed in to see them. Overnight a few nurses, *Betreuers* and doctors were permitted in; aside from them no one is allowed to go near the buildings.

*

We've managed to get some news from the buildings. None of the kids know Czech at all; we don't even know if they're Jewish, Polish or something else. We can see them a bit from the tower; this morning they went to the *Entwesung*. They look awful. It's not even possible to guess their age. They all have old, worn-down faces and tiny little bodies. Most of them have no stockings and only a few of them have shoes. They return from the *Entwesung* shaven bare; we hear they have fleas. They all have terrified eyes and resisted fearfully when shown to the baths. Were they afraid it was gas?

Yesterday afternoon they were taken away. The doctors, nurses and *Betreuers* went with them. The whole time they were quarantined they were specially cooked for and clothing was scrounged for them. The only person who managed to get in touch with them was Fredy Hirsch. Now, as a result, he's locked in a bunker at the command centre.

They've left. We never learned where they were from or where they were taken. All that's left of them is a couple of lines scrawled on the wall of the building, which we can barely decipher. And that horrible, inexplicable rumour – gas!

I spent November 10th in bed. I had a fever again. Despite that, it was a lovely birthday. I got a little present from each of the girls: a pudding from Francka, a new charm from Jindra and that's not even including Mum and Dad. Where they got it all, I don't know. So many beautiful things that I couldn't have had a nicer birthday even at home. The next day, though, was less lovely, and in time will be remembered in all of Terezín.

11 November 1943

Unfortunately, or perhaps fortunately, I didn't take part myself due to illness, and so I regret not being able to make more detailed notes.

The morning count didn't add up, and supposedly someone had run away; it was probably true, although maybe the Germans just made it up. It was necessary to undertake a full census of the inhabitants – and not in the barracks, the way it had been done before when someone was missing, but outside the ghetto. That night all the sick from the hostels and the building infirmaries were transferred to infirmaries in the barracks. Other than that, all the ghetto inhabitants, from the very youngest infants in the *Säuglingsheim* to the very oldest, were taken out to a huge meadow (the Bohušovice basin), lined up by the hundreds and left standing from daybreak until deepest darkness, constantly being rearranged and recounted, with the horrible thoughts that they would never be let back in the ghetto, that they'd be taken away and shot etc. – something they deduced from the SS men's many spiteful taunts and remarks. Although I wasn't there, I can easily imagine myself in that situation.

Others thought I was better off in my bed in Vrchlabí, although I'm not convinced. That morning was OK. Lízinka and I were sharing a bed for lack of space and we were in a pretty good mood. They came to count us too, and so we believed it was nothing more than a census. However, when by three and then by four and finally by six o'clock there was no sign that anyone else had come back, we started to worry. Our worries were the same as the people outside: the most horrible visions and finally self-reproach for not going with the rest so we could all perish together. If only we were allowed to go out in the corridor to look out of the window into the street – but that too was forbidden.

Eyes fastened on the door, ears pricked, we listened tensely for even the slightest sign of life. We waited, hunched under the bedcovers. In vain. Silence, grim and unusual, was the only response to all our questions. Will I ever see my mum and dad again? What has happened to them? Our tense, unsettled nerves, irritated by our day-long fast, gave in, and hot tears welled up in our eyes.

Around eight in the evening finally steps resounded outside. The barrack corridors came alive. The door opened and the relatives of the ill came in and told us everything. Dad came to see me too and brought me something to eat. We stayed in the hospital till morning.

No one ever returned to the gates of Terezín so happily or fell asleep so contentedly as on that night of 11th November.

❡

An international committee is coming, we hear. A huge clean-up and reorganization of the town is in progress: *Verschönerung der Stadt*. A plan is all ready as to where the committee will go and the work is being carried out accordingly. In Hamburg barracks, the third layer of bunks must be gone within 24 hours from all the rooms whose windows face on to the street. One transport has left already, true, but that is not nearly enough to free up enough spaces.

Cutting Down Bunks (1944)

*'So it happened that early one morning they came, sawed off the top bunks
and their tenants had no choice but to grab their bags and move on.'*

So it happened that early one morning they came, sawed off
the top bunks and their tenants had no choice but to grab their
bags and move on. There were no other places to go, but within
two days it had all been worked out. Some people moved into
other buildings, the rest found *Notbelags*. Mum was among
those affected; fortunately after three days of desperate searching she got a place in a bunk bed in room 211.

Christmas. We had been looking forward to it, and for a while it seemed they'd leave us alone. Even though we've had enough opportunities to get to know the Germans, we are still so naïve. There hasn't yet been a holiday where they've left us in peace. Nor would this Christmas be an exception. Aunt Ola and many of our girls left. It'll be a sad holiday.

⌒

A freshly scrubbed floor and perfectly made-up bunks. In the middle of a white tablecloth, a new, beautifully carved wooden menorah, a gigantic cake and 33 mess tin lids with slices of bread. In the corner of the room, a basket with the presents we prepared. Girls in ironed white blouses and blue skirts. Everything is ready. The Chanukah celebration begins.

The cramped loft space of building L410 filled up with the figures of girls. The first candle on the menorah flared into life and objects stretched into long, scary shadows. 360 pairs of eyes lit up. Our *Heimleiter* approached the menorah and prayed. *'Ma'oz tzur yeshu'ati . . .'* echoed quietly through the loft . . . when suddenly: 'A German's in the building!' shouted the watch, who had run up from downstairs.

The candle went out; the shadows vanished. 'Everyone into your rooms!' came the order. 'Careful, don't let them hear you.' How will it turn out? If he figures out that we were celebrating . . .! Or if he goes into our rooms and see the tables laid! This could turn into a right mess.

We'd barely got back to our room when the German – it

Chanukah in the Loft (16 January 1944)

'The cramped loft space of building L410 filled up with the figures of girls. The first candle on the menorah flared into life and objects stretched into long, scary shadows. 360 pairs of eyes lit up.'

was Lagerkommandant Burgr himself – got up to the third floor and burst into 24, our room. He went right to the table, sat down on the bench and started to question us. How was it that we had such a prettily laid table, where had we got so much bread, etc. At least we'd had the foresight to hide the menorah in time. We didn't give anything away and so he left empty-handed.

We breathed a sigh of relief, waited until they came up from downstairs to tell us he'd left the building, had our supper and gave out the presents. It was very nice and could have been even nicer if that awful man hadn't spoiled our plans.

[91]

Jaundice and typhus are out of fashion. A new illness has appeared – encephalitis. They cleared out the entire Sokol hall, formerly our typhus ward. L410 has, as always, the most cases. We've been quarantined for several days. I think they should just set up an infirmary here, otherwise the whole *Heim* will move over to the Sokol hall anyway. They've enlarged our infirmary by one room already, number 17.

The illness is running its course without too many serious cases. We're having fun with it. We know all the signs of this odd illness and we spend days examining each other. Today the girls diagnosed me with poor stomach and eye reflexes and they say my tongue is crooked. Also, I can't touch my nose with my finger when my eyes are closed.

In fact, the girls were right. On his visit today, the doctor explained what the tongue looks like when you have encephalitis. He had me stick out my tongue and that was that.

He examined me and announced it was a typical case of encephalitis. I have to go to Vrchlabí barracks for an examination.

*

At Vrchlabí they confirmed the finding. I'm in number 17. It's unbelievably disorganized and cold here. I've got my duvet and mattresses ready for disinfection. Tomorrow I go to the Sokol hall. I'm looking forward to a bath. The girls wrote that everyone has to bathe first. That will be wonderful: a bath, for the first time in three years.

*

I've been lying here over a week. There's nothing wrong with me, but no one can be released before a fortnight is up. My bed is next to Katka's. We've got nothing to do all day. I'm painting and reading a lot. Katka and I read *Quo Vadis* by Henryk Sienkiewicz together. It's a tremendously interesting book. The persecution of Christians was horrid. And it's horrid that so many centuries later similar things are happening. We also read Hora's poems; I liked them so much that I copied some of them out.

~

15 January 1944

I missed a big event: the move from Hamburg barracks. According to the letters and stories, it must have been a terrible madhouse: to move 4,000 people and all their luggage within 24 hours. Mum didn't even come this afternoon; she just wrote to say that I should be glad I wasn't there. By the time I get back, supposedly everything will be in order. Fortunately she got a pretty good place in Q610.

The doctor was here today; Pucka and I will be released. Tomorrow morning they'll bring us our *Übersiedlungschein* and we can go. Poor Francka; she was so looking forward to my coming home and now she's in the infirmary herself.

~

Pucka and I got up at half five so we could be home before the girls get up. We were surprised. The bunks have been rebuilt, covered in brown paint, the curtains dyed green and on the main wall, covered by a sheet dyed the same shade of green, there's a huge painted picture of Prague. I was silly to want to go back to Mum. Today I wouldn't trade our room 24 for anything on this earth. Except for the end of the war, but even then I'll probably miss it.

Francka has been in the infirmary almost three weeks. We were worried it would turn out to be pneumonia. Now, thank God, it's safely behind her and tomorrow she's coming home. I've got everything ready and tidied for her, so that she'll like it here. We've pasted dark red and black paper on her bunk, on the outside it's covered in pictures and on the inside are three post-cards from Prague. It feels to me like being in a little room and the postcards serve as windows. We have a view out on to Hradčany and the River Vltava. If only it were morning already and I could go fetch Francka.

~

The committee, for whose sake a transport had left and the triple-decker bunks were destroyed, left and was apparently satis-fied. They didn't see much – they were here only a half-day. But it was probably only a general review. From the *Kommandatur* new orders were sent out about the *Verschönerung*, the 'beauti-fication', which must be completed within two months.

It's funny, but it looks as if they're trying to change Terezín into a spa town. It's like in the fairy tale about the wishing-table.

In the evening the order comes, and by morning we all roll our eyes in surprise at how this or that has happened.

For three whole years it never occurred to anyone that the streets should be named anything other than L and Q. Every little child knew where Magdeburg, Jägrovka or any of the other barracks, just as any Praguer knows where Wenceslas Square is. The Germans suddenly got an idea and overnight there had to be signs hung on every corner house with the street name and at the junctions arrows pointing '*Zum Park*', '*Zum Bad*', etc. The barracks are no longer called Magdeburg, but B-five; I no longer live at L410, but at Hauptstrasse 10. All the patients were moved overnight out of the school by the *Bauhof*, which had till today been serving as our hospital; the whole building was painted, scrubbed, school desks were brought in and by morning a huge sign shone into the distance: '*Knaben und Mädchenschule*' – 'The Boys' and Girls' School'. It really does look beautiful, like a real school, except it's got no pupils or teachers. However, this drawback was fixed quite simply: a small sign announcing '*Ferien*' – 'Holidays'.

Freshly sown grass is already coming up on the town square; the middle is decorated with a huge bed of roses. The paths have been strewn with clean yellow sand and newly lacquered benches line them in two rows. The boards, whose purpose we mused over for several days, have turned into a music pavilion. We even have a café with a lovely sign, '*Kaffeehaus*'. All the shops have got new names as well. The houses too will be repainted; over on Langestrasse they have already started.

The building behind Magdeburg, which used to be for manufacture and *Glimmer*, is now the *Speisehalle*, or dining hall. Several girls are employed there heating up food. They have to wear white caps and aprons. The Sokol hall, as of this writing, has become a restaurant with carved furniture; there are plush chairs in the main hall and huge vases with flowers. On the first floor there is a library and reading room, and there are tables with coloured sunshades on the terrace.

There has been significant progress with the house painting. Several Danish hostels have received furniture. Bunks and shelves painted yellow were put up in two buildings along with blue curtains. In the park in front of the *Säuglingsheim*, they've built a luxurious pavilion with cribs and pale blue embroidered coverlets. One room has toys, a rocking horse etc. Then there's a pool, a merry-go-round and see-saws. None of us can explain why they are doing all this. Do they really care so much about this committee? Perhaps we don't even know how good the situation is.

⌒

Mum isn't working in the factory any more; she got a job in one of the *Kinderheims* as a seamstress. I'm going out to the garden again, but I applied late, so they allocated me to a different group from the other girls.

⌒

Now, instead of celebrating Mother's Day we have to pack. How many weeks were we looking forward to this; how much self-denial and self-control it took for us to save those few dozen grams of sugar and margarine for a cake. Which of us this time will be in it?

Francka is in the *Schleuse*. And several other girls beside her. The whole orphanage is in it. What did those innocent children ever do to them? I helped the kids from L318 through the *Schleuse*. Some of them can't even really speak yet. Two- and three-year-old children with transport numbers around their necks and the word *Waisenkind* – orphan – added in pencil.

I don't know who to think of first. Pucka, Doris, Hanka, Růža, Francka. It's so dead here, so quiet that it hurts. No one's bouncing above me, no one laughing, and an empty bunk next to me. My God, please let Francka out of the transport.

*

I don't know what time I fell asleep. It must have been really late; the girls were boarding on the *Hilfsdienst*'s second night shift. When we got up, it was still dark. They sent us back from the *Schleuse*; by yesterday they wouldn't take any more comers on the *Hilfsdienst* and without an armband they weren't letting anyone in. I saw them letting in people with red armbands; we cut up some shorts and made the bands ourselves.

We spent about an hour in the *Schleuse*; then they sent us away so we wouldn't get underfoot. The Germans were on a rampage and more than once they shoved someone on the train just as he was. The rest of the afternoon I stood under Francka's window and never took my eyes off the scrap of paper tied to a string. It was a sign that they were still up there and had not yet boarded. At half six the locomotive's whistle sounded and the train moved

[97]

off past Jägrovka barracks. The paper still hung from the string. Francka had been recalled.

～

From the garden, we go to Travčice to help with the hay. The journey leads past the Small Fortress and we meet groups of prisoners. Is Hanka's or Lála's father among them? Do they know anything about them? And whose fathers, husbands, sons are these? We're not allowed to speak to them.

How we'd like just to greet them, raise their hung heads and give them strength for the coming – possibly their last – days! We mustn't stop, we can't give any sign; they probably aren't allowed to look at us either. SS men with guns surround them, shouting, slapping, throwing stones. We exchange quick glances with them. We belong to you, friends, take courage, hold on a while longer. We're prisoners too, we also long to go home.

There's so much we'd like to tell them, but we mustn't . . . yet, the thought has already crossed our minds and we start to sing. Songs by Voskovec and Werich; how could the Germans understand? '*As long as I've still got my head, I'll use it to sing songs instead . . .*' Their marching improves and smiles of recognition appear on their faces. Well, comrades, heads up. '*Freedom can't be snared in chains. Chains rust, old iron can't hold us again.*'

*

Rutka's parents have been in prison for two years. She last saw her mum last year picking chestnuts, when she went into the fields with the prisoners from the Small Fortress. She had no news of her father until she saw him three weeks ago in a group of prisoners from the Small Fortress. Every day she gets up at half five and waits by the fence near the road the prisoners take to get to work. At six a.m. going, and after five p.m. on the way back. For a fortnight now Rutka has been watching in vain and letting herself get shouted at by the SS. Her dad is not with the prisoners any more. Perhaps he's been transported somewhere else, or sent for further interrogation to Prague; maybe he's ill – or has died. No one dares to mention it aloud. We console Rutka and now she's getting up at five again so as not to miss a single group.

Number 24 is a convent? They won't be saying that about us. Old maids? No one will make fun of us again. Number 24 is organizing a dance.

The invitations are ready; the cellar has been reserved; the accordion player has promised to come. We'll do a buffet in the back room of the cellar with open-faced sandwiches and lemonade. We've got everything arranged and the margarine set aside for the accordionist (he'll play all evening for half a kilo). We kind of know how to dance; Šára and Tonička are patient teachers. All that's left is to distribute the invitations.

*

It worked out marvellously. Much better than we'd expected. We'd been afraid that the boys wouldn't come, that we wouldn't know how to dance and that it would all be a huge embarrassment. But in the end everyone who was invited came and the atmosphere was superb. Some of the boys probably got their feet stepped on a bit, but by and large we got through it. Almost all evening I danced with one boy. He didn't ask practically any of the others to dance, only me. The girls are predicting a relationship, but I don't fancy him in the least. Anyway, he didn't even ask me for a date.

*

'Number 24's been corrupted,' that's what the girls from other rooms are whispering about us. For God's sake, what's the problem if some of the girls are seeing boys? Are the rest of them just sitting around at home? Did they think we'd stay a convent forever?

We had another dancing lesson. He came again and only danced with me. His name is Ota; he has curly, light brown hair and he's 25. The girls won't leave me alone about it. I make fun of them, but I don't know how long I'll be able to keep up the pretence. I'm actually starting to like him.

Mum went for an X-ray today. She has had an elevated temperature for several months and they still won't certify her as ill. She has a lingering pneumonia and should be resting. I hope they don't find anything on her lungs as a result. Dad wants her to go into hospital.

This afternoon there's a celebration on the tower; I'm really looking forward to it. Ota will probably come as well. It's been a fortnight since the second dance lesson and he still hasn't asked me on a date. Each time he meets me he stops for a while, but that's all. I just hope he comes this afternoon. If even today nothing happens, then it's probably a lost cause.

*

He was there. He walked me home and asked me on a date this evening. He's a great guy; we had a nice conversation. He's not one of those crazy boys, like the ones some of our girls date. After all, he's 25. It's a bit much for me at my age, but it doesn't really matter, since we understand each other so well. The girls are rooting for me; my act didn't work, they knew I liked him. Francka is a bit jealous, but I forgive her her silly words. Did I really insist just a month ago that I would buy myself a canary and a cat and stay an old maid? I'm looking forward to tomorrow. At half six again, at the corner of L410.

*

Beneath our windows, a band is bawling; the cleanly scrubbed pavements contrast sharply with the newly painted houses; freshly ironed curtains shine in the windows. The café is overflowing, the park benches fully occupied and the playground in front of the *Säuglingshcim* is in use for the first time. Behind Magdeburg a vehicle is waiting, but this is no *Leichenwagen*, no hearse – it's a nice, clean vehicle with bread and men in white aprons, caps and gloves. A group of the prettiest, most healthy-looking girls have been chosen from the *Landwirtschaft*, who

will bring a basket of fresh fruits, singing all the while. The
children are rehearsing one final time their joyous greeting for
'Uncle Rahm', turning up their noses at the snack they are
offered. '*Schon wieder Sardinen?*' – 'Sardines again?' Today we'll
have two bread rolls and pâté for supper, tomorrow there will
be meat for dinner. The menu has been written for the whole
week ahead, and of course for last week too. Everything is ready;
the ghetto guards are running madly here and there to make
sure they let everyone know in time. We're just waiting until
the first cars from the International Committee appear on the
road from Bohušovice and the comedy can begin.

The Arrival of the International Red Cross Committee (1944)

*To give the impression that the Jews in Terezín were well
looked after, everything was thoroughly cleaned, brightened up
and arranged like a stage set. The committee was duped
and believed that everything was in the best of order.*

I've been transferred to Kréta. I've wanted it for a long time, but now I'm not so happy about it. I don't know how I'm going to fit everything in. Mum has been in the hospital since yesterday. In Kréta we work from six to half six, with an hour break. So two hours more than I'd done up till now. At noon we have a lesson and then in the evening from eight to nine we have maths. At least the people living in Mum's room in Q610 are nice and will help me cook something. Then I can take it to Gran and Dad when he's got the evening shift. On the other hand, in Kréta I'll be able to 'sluice' things more often and besides, every other day I'll have a *Zusatz* – a supplement – and every week ¾ of a loaf of bread and two pâtés. I've got to get hold of these things myself now that Mum can't sew. Today we got a package, too, so I hope it might work out.

If only Heinl didn't carry on so. It's his fault that no one wants to join the *Landwirtschaft*. He guards us like a madman; every day he catches someone. Everyone knew his motorcycle and the moment they heard it they were on their guard. So he came up with a new method of silent skulking. Now he rides a bicycle and watches us from the opposite ramparts with a telescope. Now that I've finally got into Kréta, it might turn out to be impossible to take things at all. But regardless of how things are, I have to get Mum some vegetables.

*

It has been possible to 'sluice' things, but we're watched awfully closely. Today Heinl beat one boy for a single cucumber peel found tossed in the greenhouse. Almost all of us had something on us, but evidently he was satisfied with a blow and a mild punishment: by evening we had to level the fields along the fence. We have to be very careful bringing things in, but outside we can stuff ourselves to bursting. At the moment we've mostly got cucumbers; I eat them with bread, salt, even sugar – I'm utterly sick of them. The carrot situation is pretty bad; the field is right by the road, where Heinl can appear at any moment. However, I'm getting more experienced. I have a new skirt for gardening, very frilly, and the gendarmes are by and large good-natured. Except for Heinl, but he's got eyes everywhere.

⌒

Today it's exactly five weeks from that celebration at the tower – five weeks since our first date. People might say it's a ridiculously short time, but can one really compare time here with what it is outside? Does our life have anything in common with the rest of the world? We're only separated from it by a couple of ramparts, but isn't it something else that broke the bonds connecting us with them? When Terezín's gates open one day, once the barbed wire is torn down and the ramparts levelled, will we be able to walk on in life alongside those who stayed outside and went their own uninterrupted way through life?

Five Sundays, no more. How close we grew in those few weeks. The thing that binds us here to each other also deepens the gulf between us and those from whose midst we were violently ripped.

It was not just five weeks, but five times seven long days, when there was not an hour without some emotional tension. Hunger, filth, illnesses, epidemics and that horrible fear from the constant threat of deportation. When will there be an end to all this? What is the political situation? If it were at least possible to believe the news here, but it's all half-invented, twisted and embellished, always those stupid, optimistic *bonkes*, rumours.

It's impossible to talk with Mum about these matters; she's always snowed under with work and trying to scrape together enough food. Dad is worn out after a full day at the office and if he doesn't have the evening shift he's happy to be able to relax a bit after work. There's no talking with the girls about these things. Except a little bit with Francka. But now I have Ota, with whom I can have long, intelligent debates.

Ota was in Lípa for two years before Terezín. He tells awful tales from there. It was only a work camp, but the treatment was similar to a concentration camp. He's all alone here. He hasn't had a mother since he was twelve; his father he lost at twenty. Out of four siblings, two are in Poland and only one sister is for now still at home; she married an Aryan. Before he was expelled from school he studied chemistry; he has two semesters to go. Even here he's constantly lugging his textbooks around. He works in the laundry room as a stoker. His shifts alternate; he prefers the night shift, because next to the laundry room is a fruit garden and he can 'sluice' apples there. Every evening I get one and he's always bringing me food and forcing it on me. I really don't like taking it from him; he's got so little himself other than a bit of bread, margarine and sugar, which he gets for odd jobs. He looks miserable, and yet the little he has, he shares with me. A wonderful fellow!

I stayed home today; yesterday I'd had a temperature. There's nothing wrong with me, but the doctor wrote me a sick note.

And what of it – for a month I clocked in every day, I can play hookey just this once. If only the *Toranut* girls were here with supper already. By 7 o'clock I have to nip over to Mum's, then a bit of time with Ota and at 8 o'clock it's maths.

⌐

Night, ¼ to 2

Ugh, these revolting bedbugs! It's impossible to sleep. There are only six of us left here; the rest have moved out to the courtyard and the corridor. We have the light on, but it doesn't help. That's why they say 'as nosy as a bedbug'. They crawl around the walls, across the duvets, all over your body, fall from the bunks right into your face. Up till now they've more or less left me alone, but today they seem to have got a taste for my blood. I don't even bother killing them any more; I sacrificed a whole stack of paper to them and still can't bring myself to squash them with my hands. We compete to see who can catch more of them. I'm losing – so far I've only got 30, Hanka is in the lead: 66 personal and 33 community ones, caught on the floor, walls, tables and benches. Three more days till disinfection. If I'm not quick enough to grab a place outside tomorrow (even next to the toilets, as long as it's not in here), that will be three nights without sleeping a wink.

*

During the disinfection the girls are staying over in Hamburg; I'm in Mum's free bunk. I've got a temperature again, but this afternoon I have to go to work. I hear we're loading carrots and I can't let an opportunity like this slip by.

*

Mum is out of hospital; there's only a small shadow left on her lungs. Still, she has to conserve her strength. Yesterday we got a package, so at least there's something to help her convalesce.

*

Back in L410, but not in 24 any more. Despite our loud protests and requests they moved us to 27. Our initial prejudice against this *Heim* is subsiding and it seems like it might even be nicer here than our old home – but still, we were and will always remain number twenty-four.

There are only 21 of us here, not a single empty bunk. I've got a place by the window again in a single; Francka is next to me, underneath me is Rutka, and Hanka's on the third level. The boys are making us some shelves to share, for our shoes, dishes and food. The suitcases are up in the loft, clothes are in the wardrobe in the corridor. Nothing must be under the bunk – no rubbish, everything in its place. We entrusted Ota with dyeing our curtains and tablecloths.

It'll be fine here; if only we were done with cleaning already. But enough writing for now – and hey ho, on to painting the bunks . . .

17 September 1944

Ironed curtains, bunks all made up the same, and it's clean, ever so clean here and all around the building. The girls are hurrying to get dressed (everyone's in white blouses and blue skirts today) and fix supper. We whisper among ourselves – really, you don't even dare speak aloud, that's how beautiful and festive it is today. It's the evening of the holiday Rosh Hashanah.

*

A competition for the cleanest, best-decorated and prettiest *Heim*. We won. I think we rightfully deserve the first prize. Number twenty-seven was truly exemplary. Not only in looks, but also in behaviour.

A party is in the works; every room will contribute a number. We've already got a programme and are rehearsing diligently every day.

*

This afternoon we hoed the celery; I brought back three bunches. The spinach is ever so slowly coming out; the lettuce hearts are coming along . . .

That was a week ago, yesterday, and this afternoon. An hour ago Ota and I went outside; we had no idea . . .

And no? Oh, girls, I sit here among you – no, I won't tell you anything. Rehearse your lines, laugh, play, be merry – at least for today. Once I tell you – maybe you'll never laugh again. Sing, frolic – how much I'd like to join you, but now I know, so I won't be able to.

An hour ago we were on our way back from a walk over by Magdeburg. Cheerful, carefree. Clumps of people were standing in front of the building. 'Five thousand men.'

Farm Work *(13 March 1943)*

There were advantages to cultivating vegetables for the Germans. One laboured outside the ghetto in the fresh air, and in spite of prohibitions one could manage to smuggle in some food or at least eat something surreptitiously.

I didn't catch Dad in the office. Still, I didn't need him to confirm it. The corridors of Magdeburg speak for themselves. The booming footfalls, rustling clothes, roaring ghetto guards, slamming doors, and hysterical crying always sound the same and mean the same thing.

Five thousand, all men. Supposedly for work, to build a new ghetto. Somewhere near Königstein. Two and a half thousand tomorrow, two and a half the day after. Uncle Jindra is in the first, Dad and Ota in the second.

*

The *Schleuse* is in Hamburg. Jindra boards early morning. I have to help Ota finish packing his bags. Dad is ready. He probably wouldn't even have to go; he could get himself recalled. He might get out, but that wouldn't be him. 'Ask on my own behalf? Five thousand are going, why shouldn't I go as well? Someone else would have to go in my place.'

⌒

28 September 1944

Yom Kippur. I'm fasting and no one had better tell me it's point-less. Not this year, not right now.

The first group are still in the *Schleuse*. The second have not had to board yet. The train carriages haven't arrived. I'm fasting and – it's probably foolish – I believe there will be a miracle.

The carriages have come, the first two and a half thousand are gone, but the second deportation is not boarding. Rumour is they're having to combine – no trains, supposedly, the tracks are broken; maybe they won't go. The optimists are unpacking their luggage.

*

9 p.m.

A chill breeze blows through the open windows into the room. Outside it's quiet, here and there a cart rattles, a recalled person returns from the *Schleuse*.

Number twenty-seven today. Unmade beds, shelves over-turned, ripped and darned socks, men's shirts and handkerchiefs hung over the stove, underneath it washbasins with water to be poured out. Suitcases under the bunks, rucksacks on the floor, there a pot of margarine, a piece of bread.

Each of us has someone in it – a father, brother, some of us both. This is the former number twenty-four, which only three days ago was rehearsing a play; these are the girls who could laugh so heartily.

We sit around the table; Milan, Miluška's boyfriend, and Ota are here as well. We're singing. Folk songs, Terezín parodies. The boys sing too, and loudly, drowning us out, cracking jokes. The girls are laughing, and I laugh with them. Then suddenly silence, and again the boys rescue the situation with their humour. For God's sake, be quiet now, don't pretend, you're deceiving us and yourselves as well. Don't laugh, it only makes things worse. This is what you call a good mood? Gallows humour, that's what it is; don't play the hero. Maybe I'm a coward, but my tears are more sincere than your laughter. Let me cry . . .

*

The boys have left; we're in bed, no one is asleep. The light is on; it helps the night pass faster.

*

The darkness is broken by the first rays of daylight. It's still peaceful outside. We wait. Any moment the carriage wheels might rumble – and then all hope is gone; it means the end is here.

⌒

29 September 1944

The train carriages are here, the second transport is starting the *Schleuse*. Mum is quickly getting supper ready, so Dad can have one last real meal. Ota is here too, this whole week of transports he's been having supper with us. I stuff myself with food; I don't know what I'm eating. Does it even matter? I swallow mouthfuls; I'm not hungry, but with each spoonful I swallow a single tear. There is not enough food; there are far more tears.

Dad and Ota are rolling cigarettes in the Russian style, filling them with tea and laughing. Gallows humour again!

A quarter to six; we have to go.

Roll-ups laid aside on the bench, and laughter abandoned along with them. All three of us used to sit here, every evening – not for long, only this last three-quarters of a year. This was our best time at Terezín, our happiest days here.

If only the war had ended already . . . it would have been too beautiful.

So here we sit today for the last time. From tomorrow, Mum and I are alone. And you, Dad? His hand tosses the still-smouldering cigarette away, clutches me to him and Mum on the other side. We can't hold back the tears; we've stored up too many of them this past week and we can't resist them any longer. With my head pressed to Dad's chest I can distinctly hear the beating of his heart. Halting, sad, like the mood this evening. Oh, Dad, if only your hands were so strong that no one could rip me from their embrace. I hear your heart; I feel it trembling and yet its beats are firm and resolved. Resolved to face the battle that awaits it, ready for the wounds it will receive, bleeding from a wound that struck it in the most vulnerable of places: a farewell. And still it beats, it will beat and must beat on! Our hearts will be with him; they will fight and suffer with him, hope and believe. And just as ours do, his will beat for us . . .

*

Hamburg, third courtyard. Half one at night. We're boarding. We have white dresses and *Hilfsdienst* armbands; we can accompany them as far as the gates. Ota must already be on the train. What a shame; I couldn't even help him with his luggage, or I wouldn't have got back from the second courtyard

'We didn't know each other for long, but . . . they were wonderful times. I'll remember them happily, and don't you forget them either. You know the address to come to after the war. Maybe we'll meet again.' He gave me his photo to remember him by. On the back side he wrote a verse from Nezval's *Manon Lescaut*: 'When the key rattles the dark seminary gates, don't leave me there, come stroke my face.' A kiss, a squeeze of my hand, then he helped me climb over the fencing. Now he's in the train and in a few hours he'll be leaving . . .

We approach the gate quickly; forty people more, now thirty. Dad takes his luggage from us, here it goes again . . . Twenty people in front of us. What's this? They're closing the gates . . . 'Everyone back to the barracks!' No more boarding; they don't have enough train carriages. Is it possible; will they really get to stay? Perhaps a miracle has occurred . . .

Five hundred women have to volunteer to join the thousand men left. Mum wants to come forward; Dad won't let her. He says he knows what he's doing. But we want to go, Mum and I. After all, if he's going, it's our responsibility to go with him. No, it's his responsibility to see that we stay here.

All the men talk that way. Why isn't it obvious that we want to go with them? Would they let us go alone if it was the other way round? They won't let us; they were promised that we'd be spared from any future transports.

⌐

1 October 1944

I can still see him standing on the steps, waving, smiling . . . Oh, God, what sort of smile was that? I've never seen him like that before. He probably meant it to be a laugh, but all that came out was a failed grimace. The corners of his mouth twitched oddly. 'Daddy!'

He's gone, lost in the crowd among the rest of them. Mum and I looked in vain for him from the window. But he was nowhere to be seen. He probably couldn't get out past the luggage. But his stretched lips, that forced attempt at a smile. Daddy, why wouldn't you let us volunteer? You didn't believe you were going to build a new ghetto! Your eyes glittered strangely and your hand shook as you pressed me to yourself for the last time. What did it mean? Goodbye, or farewell? Daddy, did you believe we'd ever meet again?

The Departure of a Transport (4 April 1943)
Ghettowache *(ghetto guards) form a chain to separate those leaving and prevent others from reaching them.*

3 October 1944

This afternoon they're bringing the summonses for another
transport. 1,500 family members of those who left. Of course
they promised them that their families would be spared. So that
was just another big lie. We could have left straight away yesterday and at least we would have been together. Who knows if
they'll send us to the same place. If we'd had our way, we'd
already be gone, but Dad didn't want it. And now we'll be in
different places. We're almost certain to be in it. And if not today,
then tomorrow or the day after. There'll be no respite. I'll go
and see Mum; maybe she knows something already. I hope we
were right not to volunteer – that's fate and there's nothing that
can be done about it. Maybe we'd have had second thoughts one
day if things had turned out badly.

*

I'm ending my Terezín diary here. One stage of my life has
ended. Only the memories remain.

I'm opening a new notebook; I'll start to fill its empty pages
tomorrow. Will I see this next one through to the end as well?

3. Auschwitz, Freiberg, Mauthausen, Home

4 October 1944

We might have been able to get out of it, but we didn't want to. Since we're in it, we're going. In this case it's best to leave things as you find them. We've been allowed to take all our luggage – a good sign. Maybe they were right and we're following the men. I'm looking forward to it; perhaps I'll see Dad by the end of the day.

It's 12 o'clock; the train has left the station. We were lucky to get on the train. We're in the last carriage. It's a good thing we went out to the courtyard early; there was a mêlée at the gate. I feel as if my back's broken. It wasn't easy pushing my way through starting at four a.m. with a rucksack on my back. It's never happened in a transport before that people fought so hard to get on the train. Today's transport is different from the others. We're following our men. I'm following Dad and Ota.

I wonder if a *Transportleitung* will come and help us with our luggage, like when we arrived at Terezín? Maybe Dad or Ota will be at the station. They'll be surprised to see us. We should be there soon – Königstein, they said, it must be close already. We've been travelling about six hours.

*

For God's sake, aren't we there yet? We've been travelling all night. That's not possible. Königstein isn't even that far away. What's happened – the train's stopped for a while. No, now it's flying onwards – that was a siren, there must be an air raid somewhere. What if it hits here? We're in Germany now, there are air raids here. Why is the train going so horribly fast?

*

It's getting light out. Where are we now? We've just passed through a station. Katowice. My God, that's the Polish border. Where are they taking us? The front's in Poland now. Could it be to Birkenau? But we heard it had been wound up, that transports weren't going there any more. So where are we headed? Are our men there? If so, then it doesn't matter where we go, so long as we stay together.

*

We've been travelling for twenty-four hours. Where, only God knows. We're all starting to get nervous. People were saying all sorts; listen to them and the front must be far behind us, and yet we've been travelling across Poland for half a day now and there's no sign of it. Now the train has started to slow. Could we finally be there? I don't want to believe it – I'd started to think this trip would never end. We're getting close, definitely – you can see buildings over there. And so many of them – it's a huge camp. I can see people, but what are they wearing? It looks like pyjamas, and they've all got the same ones.

My God, those are prisoners' clothes! Where have they taken us?! This is a concentration camp! There are some men working over there, stacking boards. Why is that man beating them so hard? It must hurt horribly, he took a cudgel to them. How can he be so cruel? He isn't even a German – he's also in a striped jumper, but he's got a band on his arm.

I must have been wrong; we can't be stopping here. Why would they take us to a concentration camp? It's not as if we've done anything. It's horrible how they treat people here. I can't watch; it makes me ill. He's walloped another one, an old man. What a stinker; he's barely twenty. Shame on him; that man could be his father and to treat him that way. He kicked him again till the poor old man staggered.

So that's what a concentration camp looks like; I could never imagine it. People have been living this way for several years. And we complained about Terezín. That was an absolute paradise compared to this.

What's this? The train has stopped. A whole group of striped people is running towards us. Is there anyone among them from Terezín? Maybe they've come to help with our baggage. Perhaps Dad's among them. But no, they've probably just come to see what sort of train this is. We're not getting off here, surely? Or – why didn't it occur to me earlier? – this is Auschwitz, of course. Birkenau is nearby, maybe the trains don't go there, so we'll have to walk that bit. Definitely, that's the way it is. This is Auschwitz, the concentration camp, and we're going to Birkenau, the work camp.

*

The carriage next to us is already alighting. Why so much noise over there? They're banging on our door. I suppose it's our turn now. Why are there so many SS men outside? Are they all here to guard us? Where would we run to? It would be pointless anyway. We're in it; there's no helping us.

'Everyone out! Leave your luggage where it is! *Alle heraus, schneller!!!*' Leave everything here, hand luggage too? Why are they shouting so much, what's with the spiteful smiles? They're grabbing everyone by the wrist; what are they looking for, watches? If only they wouldn't yell at us so much, and what do those grimaces and comments mean? They're treating us as if we belong in that concentration camp. One woman just got a slap for trying to take a loaf of bread with her. Is this Birkenau?

Why is my throat so scratchy? I don't want them to know how I feel.

Stupid eyes – why are they smarting? I mustn't cry! For all the world, not now!! '*Alles da lassen!*' – 'Leave everything as is!' – '*Schneller, heraus!!!*'

*

They sort us into two groups. One – older women and mothers with young children – goes to the left; the other goes to the right. 'Sick people shouldn't say anything,' hushed voices repeat; 'you're all healthy,' one of the ones in prisoner's clothes whispers in Czech just behind me. A Czech, then. The queues in front of us move; soon it will be our turn. As long as they leave me and Mum together. Surely they can't separate us if I say we belong together. Or will it be better not to say we're together? Probably; maybe they deliberately wouldn't let us stay together if they knew how much it mattered to us.

They're even taking mothers away from their children. I know that girl there; she's going to the right and her mum's going left. But the mum's quite old; she's got grey hair. My mum still looks

[120]

young. But . . . maybe I look too much like a child? Maybe they'll ask me how old I am. Should I tell the truth? Fifteen; no, that's too little – they'd send me left and separate me from Mum. I'd better say I'm older, maybe eighteen. Do I look it? Sure, maybe they'll believe me.

The queue is getting shorter; the group of five in front of us has gone. Oh Lord, I pray to you, leave me and Mum together. Don't let them send us each a different way.

Two more people and it's our turn. For God's sake, what if he asks me what year I was born? Quickly: 1929 and I'm fifteen, so if I'm eighteen . . . 29, 28, 27, that makes 1926. Mum is standing in front of the SS man, he's sent her to the right. Lord, let us stay together! '*Rechts!*' the SS man snarled at me and pointed the way with his finger. Praise be, we're both on the same side. Thank you, God, a thousand thanks for making it work out.

⌒

First they led us to the baths, where they took from us everything we still had. Quite literally there wasn't even a hair left. I've sort of got used to the shaven heads, but the first impression was horrid. I didn't even recognize my own mother till I heard her voice. But so what, hair will grow back, it's not such a tragedy, as long as we survive. I don't hold out much hope. As soon as we got here, they held us up with a long speech, of which I remember nothing beyond the first sentence, which was plenty: '*Ihr seid in Vernichtungslager!*' *You are in an extermination camp*. Upon which they drove us here, into this building, on to bunks from which we are not allowed to move.

Hungarian Jews on the selection ramp at Auschwitz, May/June 1944. Those deemed fit to work were sent to the right; those sent to the left were immediately gassed.

I'm seriously hungry; we've not eaten since morning, it must be seven o'clock already, but it doesn't look as if we'll be getting any supper. Who knows, maybe they won't feed us at all and will leave us to die of hunger. If only we'd eaten that pâté on the train; we were saving it for Dad, so we'd have something to give him right away.

My God, we're such idiots, what were we thinking? 'You're following your men to a new ghetto.' And we believed them. Some people even volunteered to come. That's why they let us take all our luggage. A nice pile of things they can put in their warehouse today.

We're better off going to bed and sleeping off our hunger. Maybe they'll leave us alone for today. Figuring out how to fit ten into a space for four will be a problem, of course, but we'll manage somehow. If we all lie on our sides in one direction, it might work. We have three covers (that's not really the right word, but I can't find another term for the filthy rags that perhaps at one time used to be covers) that we have to share; we'll put our clothes under our heads – so yes, it'll work. We won't be comfortable, but after all the events and afflictions of the last twenty-four hours I'm so tired that I think I could sleep well even on these bare boards.

What must the girls in the *Heim* be doing? Francka, Šáry and the others? Will they remember me? And what about my lovely bunk? I won't see out the end of the war on it now.

*

So they're not letting us die of hunger. By this I don't mean that there was plenty of tasty food, not by any reckoning, but it doesn't matter, the main thing is that there was something at all.

Early in the morning came the wake-up call, after which each bunk received a pot with scrapings in it. They said that we're new here so there was no more left for us. I was utterly miserable. If that's how they're going to feed us, then it's the end for us. Although it wasn't at all edible – cold, thick and bitter – we forced it down. Partially to fill our stomachs with something, anything, and also because we were afraid that they would punish us for leaving food.

After breakfast was roll-call, where they counted us, left us standing there for an hour, maybe two, I don't know exactly, because I don't have a watch – in any case it was endless. Why I don't know; apparently it's part of the daily programme. They only let us back in the building once it seemed to them that we were sufficiently tired and frozen through and through. It's only October, but it was freezing cold standing there at four in the morning (it must have been around then, it was still completely dark), almost naked, for the rags they dressed us in can't be called clothes, our bare feet stuck in Dutch clogs (sometimes only one clog, if you're not clever and energetic enough to clamber down from the bunk in time and there aren't enough to go round) – and the worst thing of all, with a shaven head; that's the part that gets coldest.

Besides that, this Polish climate is awfully odd. During the day the sun beats down till people faint from the heat, while in the early morning it freezes worse than at home in December. I have to laugh when I remember how Mum always got mad when I wouldn't want to put on a cap or long stockings in winter. If I ever get home again, I will never wear anything on my head till the day I die.

No sooner had we crawled (in the true sense of the word; there are no ladders here like there were at Terezín) back on our bunks and wrapped our numb legs and hands in rags than it was time to get up again, from whence we went to the latrine and the *Waschraum*. Everything went by at such a pace that it was absolutely impossible to use either of these two rooms. We'd barely taken two steps inside and the guards were chasing us out again, using cudgels and suchlike.

Marching at a pace quick enough to lose your clogs in the mud so abundant here, we returned to the building. Shortly thereafter they brought soup – called *zupa* here – not too tasty, with everything possible (and impossible) floating in it. Rotten

[124]

turnip, corn cobs, bits of frozen marrow, stalks and beetroot, which gave the mixture a pinkish colour. As earlier that morning, five to ten people ate from a single pot. That didn't help the taste, because we don't even have spoons. Many people turned up their noses or didn't even eat, but not me. You have to eat – doesn't matter how or what. Like the proverb 'A good pig eats everything', I stuffed myself as full as I could. I used my teeth and my hands – just like the others who understand what's what and don't give themselves airs.

In the evening there was roll-call again, when bread rations were given out – a quarter-loaf of dark rye for each person and a spoonful of jam. We have no knives, so we just broke off bits and spread the jam with the crust. Mum and I hid one portion for the next morning and ate the other for supper. One of the guards gave me a handkerchief – I was surprised, since they're all such pigs. She saw Mum covering my head with her bare hands and it must have awakened a bit of human kindness in her; the rest aren't susceptible.

*

I'm so angry with myself; I let myself be waited on like a small child and I just sob all day. I can't help it; everything here is so horrible. Bedtime is drawing near and I'm already good for nothing. Lying unmoving in one position until morning. Last night I didn't even wake up once, but this morning I was all bruised, my bones felt as if they'd been broken, dreadful. You can't sleep well on a hard surface and now here it is again. Oh, God, why are you punishing us like this? '*Ruhe, alle schlafen, schneller!*' – 'Silence, everyone to sleep, hurry up!' The block warden patrols the middle of the building and the guards tear about shouting like madwomen. '*Schlafen, schneller!*' The lights have gone out.

*

The morning was the same as yesterday except that they would not let us back from the latrines into block 9, where we'd come from, and sent us into another block two further down. After lunch they moved us somewhere else again, where we spent several trying moments. It was already *Lagerruhe*, camp curfew; outside it was dark and suddenly . . . gunfire, a shout, the noise of footsteps fleeing and another shot . . . A wail, frightened voices, the door to our barracks opened slightly and several childish figures, their eyes wide with fear, slipped through the small crack. They spread out and clambered into the bunks among the others. Mum and I were sitting on the third level and three of them climbed into the bottom bunk.

We stared, frozen, into space and only a while later, from a few fearfully whispered words, did we understand what was going on. They were moving children from our camp over to the other side. The other side! People talk about it so much; the guards use it to threaten us over every silly thing, but as far as what it looks like there and what happens, I can't find out. A mysterious phrase – the other side – that makes everyone shiver. I understand it to mean gas . . .

Now clattering again, angry male voices, cries, more gunfire and loud wailing. The thud of heavy, hobnailed boots right in front of the building. They're coming here! They saw the children running to us! We are sitting on the first bunk next to the entrance and the hidden children are beneath us. They'll find them. They'll shoot. They'll shoot all of us. It's the end! These thoughts flashed through my mind; I hugged Mum even closer and started to pray: 'God, if I must die, then at least let Mum and me die together. Don't leave me alone here. Don't let me die after Mum does. Although I don't want to die – let me live, let Mum and me survive till the war ends.'

The steps slowly faded into the distance; the crying ceased. We were safe, and the children who'd run to us were too.

Before we came here to number eighteen, they left us sitting for a while in a building where Mum found a bucket of cooked potatoes. Probably a guard forgot them there. We divided them among everyone in the bunk; there were only eight potatoes left over. But they'll be good too: we're covered in case there's another day when we don't get any bread. Yesterday with all the moving they either forgot or it happens here more frequently; I don't know. In the morning I even managed to wash my face.

Today it was horribly hot; lots of people fainted during roll-call. I learned something interesting: they have an odd way of reviving people who have fainted. No artificial breathing or dousing with cold water. At first it seemed strange to me, but I came to see that no scientific or medical procedures work better or more quickly than this simple method: slapping. Everyone comes to, immediately.

*

They allowed us to write to Terezín. There isn't much point in it; I doubt they will even send our letters and we can't write the truth in them anyway. For our address, we were told to write: 'Arbeitslager Birkenau'. From the name, no one will imagine this and won't know that it's the same as Auschwitz. Just as we had no idea from the letters that reached Terezín from here.

However, we have some agreed signs: they'll know that every-thing we write is the precise opposite. The main thing is for them to have some word from us; the question, of course, is whether the letters will get there. They also told us to write that we'll be travelling onwards for work. There's been talk of it from the moment we arrived and I kept hoping for it to happen, but now, since they've let us write about it, I don't believe it any more at all.

We lived in number eighteen for two days. One guard took a liking to me; I helped her clean up and at noon I got as a reward three pans of *zupa*. She's Polish; her name is Brochc. A really nice girl; she's not like the other guards, which is why I've become friends with her. I wouldn't have anything to do with the other ones; they're monsters – not even if they gave me a whole caul-dron of *zupa*.

If only they'd left us in number eighteen. Perish the thought – here apparently you sleep in a different place every night. They must save a lot of bread this way, because in the confusion one building always gets forgotten about, as happened to us today for the second time.

*

At noon a transport from Terezín arrived. We were waiting by the latrine when they went by. I saw Laška and Růža Vogelová;

they said their mum, Líza and Zuzka had gone to the other side. What about Rutka? She arrived with me and I've not seen her again. Rutka is shorter than I; she probably went to the left. And Mrs Spitzová and Anita too. I can't believe it's possible that none of them are still alive, or that they'll be gassed any day now. Cheerful, smiling Rutka, our little Rutka; little Líza and her tiny sister Zuzka, who was born in Terezín.

Maybe the guards are just trying to frighten us and give us the creeps. Have any of them been on the other side? Are there really gas chambers there? I look in vain towards where that awful place is supposed to be. All our questions are pointless. The only things I see, which serve as an answer, are two chimneystacks that pour smoke day and night. The crematorium, they say.

The boards wouldn't even hurt me so much, but last night was woefully bad. It started with the so-called *Entwesung*, disinfestation. I kept thinking they were going to gas us. It wasn't that bad, but I'm fed up.

We had to take off our clothes and then they left us there. The first people's turn came after two hours; some weren't done until morning. The main purpose was probably to ensure we caught a proper cold and changed our clothing. I expected I'd get some different, disinfected ones, but perish the thought! They gave them out from the same pile where we'd taken them off – of course we got someone else's and each of us got either a dress or underclothes but not both, as we'd had before.

The bathing was over in a trice. Each of us walked through some showers and finally they sprayed us with Lysol. To make sure it all went off smartly and with no fuss, there were SS watching us, fairly young snotty-nosed boys, who must have been having great fun. We didn't have towels, of course, and so there was no choice but to wriggle into our clothes wet. There would have been no point drying off anyway, because it was pouring outside and we got even wetter.

There was shooting, much more noticeable than the night before. We hear they're shelling Cracow, the front's approaching. Maybe they'll come liberate us soon. God willing.

*

This building has a block warden; she must be a real pig. She struts around like a peahen in a satin bathrobe and a nightshirt. She left one woman kneeling on the bricks for asking for permission to use the toilet. Pig – well, there's no other word for her. Even that's too nice, the comparison is an insult to pigs everywhere.

They didn't even give us blankets, only a single paper-like coverlet made of straw to cover five people. But now I'm not even chilled; I've not caught the flu and I don't think anyone will even catch cold. You can withstand a lot, much more than you think. It's almost unbelievable: Mum just got over pneumonia and since we've been here she's completely stopped coughing.

*

A little while after roll-call (we were allowed to stay on our bunks; they just counted our legs – perhaps they felt a little bit sorry since we froze all night) an SS guy flew into the building; he must have been about sixteen. '*Alle nackt ausziehen und heraus!*' – 'Everyone strip naked and outside!' Again they divided us into two groups. Another moment of nervousness; would we stay together? It worked out OK. No sooner had we pulled our

Counting Legs (1945/6)

'. . . *we were allowed to stay on our bunks; they just counted our legs –*
perhaps they felt a little bit sorry since we froze all night . . .'

clothes back on than they were herding us onwards. People in
the building gazed at us sorrowfully and it occurred to me that
they were taking us to be gassed. I tried every which way to
banish this thought. Everyone said we were going to be put
to work and we should be happy. All pointless – gas, the gas
chambers, went round and round in my head and wouldn't
stop.

We went through the gate of C-camp, then a bit of the path
ran right alongside the *Mänerlager*, the men's camp; I kept an
eye out for Dad – perhaps he was in one of the buildings, he
must have been sent here, to Auschwitz. But I quickly gave up

any hope I'd had of actually finding him. It would have been an incredible coincidence: we were walking so fast that there was no time to look round. It was all we could do to keep up with the pace and not lose our clogs in the mud. Then came another order: '*Stehen bleiben!*' – 'Halt!'

At that moment a huge downpour began. We were soaked to the skin in no time. We clung tightly to each other to protect our bodies from the weather. Our clothes stuck to us and the dye from them ran down our legs in little streams.

Despite all our curses, appeals and prayers, the rain didn't stop until late in the afternoon. The setting sun briefly landed on us and the water began to evaporate; we disappeared completely in the steam. Only after that did our teeth start to chatter and goosebumps appeared.

It was already getting dark when the line began to move again a bit. They wrote everyone down; for safety's sake I said 1926 again and Mum took four years off, so the age difference wouldn't be so great. We've not told anyone that we're mother and daughter; supposedly it's better that way.

The baths were very similar to yesterday's *Entwesung*, just a lot bigger; they called it a sauna. There was awfully little time for bathing; we didn't get a chance to wash at all. After bathing we waited in an empty room with the windowpanes bashed out. Towels would have been unnecessary; the draught dried us off completely. Everything took place beneath the strict gaze of the youngest SS men.

I got incredibly lucky when clothes were distributed. I have a dress with long sleeves, high shoes (they don't match, but that's OK, everyone's are like that) and a coat with padding. It comes down to my ankles and can be buttoned at the neck. I have never been, nor will I ever again be, so pleased with anything as I am with this coat. I'm so beautifully warm in it; I'm so happy.

*

Late that night we got into a train (covered cattle cars). At the camp gates we each got a loaf of bread, a bit of margarine and a slice of salami. I tore into the bread as we walked and while boarding. We hadn't eaten since yesterday evening. Now I've got the salami into me as well and I'm feeling good again. Mum and I wrapped the margarine into a bit of the lining of my coat and hung it on a nail. We also tore off a bit of the padding for our heads.

We're sitting on the floor; there are fifty of us in the middle of this car. Somehow we have to lie down to sleep. There's something hard behind me, a board or something; it's pressing into me horribly, but I can't stand up now. In the morning I'll have to fix it. I'm curious where we're going. Supposedly it's a good transport. We'll see; it could be like with Königstein again. But nowhere could it be worse than here. At least I hope not.

After a twenty-four hour ride they decanted 500 of us at the station in Freiberg. The rest travelled on. After a bit of a walk, we came to a huge building. It's probably a factory. An SS man was waiting – all signs indicate he's the camp director; they call him *Unterscharführer* – with lots of *Aufsehers*, overseers. He read

[133]

out the roll to see if we were all here, told us how to behave and then divided us into rooms. It was already late at night.

We couldn't believe our eyes. We're going to live here. In a proper building with walls, not in those awful shacks like at Auschwitz. To sleep on proper bunks and not in those horrid cages. Always two and two on one. I've got an advantage in that I'm with Mum and don't have to sleep with a stranger. We crawled up on to the third row. It's lovely lying here – it's so soft, and so warm. There's even central heating. We were really lucky to get out – this certainly won't be a bad camp.

*

I've never slept as well as last night. It was only on straw, with my coat folded under my head, but to me it felt like lying on a feather bed. I'm so happy that we've ended up here. I feel like a human being again. We were each allocated a coverlet (there are three now on each bunk), a towel for every two of us, and everyone got a bowl, mug and spoon. The last makes me happiest; we don't have to eat with our hands like animals any more; we're like people again.

We all live on the same corridor. Supposedly there are some Polish women on the second floor, but we're not allowed to go up there – or off this hallway at all. Still, that doesn't matter. We have everything we need here. Even flush toilets and a tiled washroom. If only there were running water. I'd like to have a wash; I think the grime will never come off. We don't have any soap and the whole time we were in Auschwitz, even at bathing hours, there was no time for washing. Also, we've not had any liquids for 24 hours and the exhaustion after the trip . . . I am terribly thirsty.

*

I fainted at roll-call. Thirst is dreadful, worse than hunger. Mum wiped the drains in the washroom; there were a few drops of water there, and so she revived me. The water began to run that night; I heard it and went for a drink. Immediately I felt better.

At noon there was marrow soup; there were even pieces of meat in it. Everyone could have as much as she wanted. As long as they keep feeding us this way, then we'll be able to survive. If only Dad is doing as well.

We've been here for a fortnight, but it seems like forever. Every day we have marrow soup – a litre per person, not as much as we want, like that first day. It's nothing but water and an hour later the hunger is back. We're allocated 400 grams of bread, but the guards are horrendous cheats.

We should already be working, but there have been a few cases of scarlet fever, so we're quarantined. We can't even go out in the corridor; we've not moved from this room for a fortnight. If we could at least be in our bunks, I'd sleep all day; at night it's impossible due to the bedbugs. In my whole life I've never seen as many as there are here; Terezín was nothing. They crawl around the walls even in broad daylight. During the day we have to have our bunks made perfectly and sit elsewhere. We sit on the ground; there isn't room for everyone on the chairs. Our daily programme consists of waiting for food and endless boredom. If no more scarlet fever breaks out, we'll go to work tomorrow.

We're working in a building here that is a factory for aeroplanes. We work in shifts, from 12 to 12. Last week we started at noon; that was OK. This week we start at midnight; we never get enough sleep. We come home at noon, then we stand at roll-call for an hour while our soup gets completely cold. After lunch we go to wash; it's three o'clock before we get to bed. We sleep for an hour and a half and then bread is distributed. By the time they give out the *Zulags* (the 'bonuses' consist of 10 grams of margarine and a spoonful of jam) it's six o'clock and at eight they bring round coffee. Between the two distributions the guards make such a racket that it's impossible to sleep. After coffee we sleep two hours and at 10 o'clock it's wake-up. We have to be ready within half an hour and lined up for roll-call.

*

If we have to stay on this shift any longer, I don't know how we'll survive. The hunger's a lot worse on this shift too. We get dinner just before bed and the bread has to last us for the whole twelve hours at work – and the work is so stupid at that. The whole time we are not allowed to sit down and yet there's nothing at all to do. That's the worst thing, because we can't let it be known and we have to keep pretending we're working. We're polishing aeroplane parts, horribly annoying. You stand in one place, doing the same motions with your hands. It's also terribly unhealthy to be swallowing iron filings the whole time and we never get out in the fresh air.

*

I thought something would happen on 28 October, but there wasn't even an air raid. In a fortnight it'll be my birthday. If only the end would come by then. That would be a present.

❧

Now the day shift works from six to six. However, I'm not so lucky; our particular hall works till eight. It's still the same monotonous polishing. Mum was transferred to the second floor, assembling small wings.

*

Every morning at roll-call, Šára (that's what we call the *Unterscharführer*, or sometimes Uša as well) finds an excuse to slap someone. I'm unlucky enough that it always happens right nearby. At first it made me ill, but now I'm past caring about such things. It was worse when one time he remembered that someone had left her papers in the *Waschraum* and he didn't give us any bread. Otherwise I'm becoming completely indifferent to everything.

❧

'They're in Görlitz already and Bautzen, 80 km from here. By New Year it will all be over. A peace conference is meeting. The newspapers admit Cologne is gone.' All that was making the rounds here, but for now, the only fact is that it's a week after Christmas, the soup is getting weaker and weaker and we're down to 300 grams of bread.

We hear we'll be moving into real buildings.

The work halls are completely unheated. The floor here is cement; our shoes are shredded and we have no stockings. Šára has forbidden us to wear coats. We couldn't bear the cold and so we took the stuffing (for those of us who happened to have greatcoats) and the linings from our coats and made foot-rags, kerchiefs for our heads and vests for underneath our dresses. Today Šára took them all away. So now we've got thin coats and we're still freezing. The cold is horrible, maybe even worse than thirst and hunger.

*

I was at home for three days with a 40-degree fever and tonsillitis. I fainted twice in the ward. Today they certified me fit for work again.

We've been afraid of it for so long, and now it's here. We're moving into the buildings. Outside in the fresh air for the first time in four months. It was terribly cold: a snowstorm. The factory is about half an hour from here. I thought I wouldn't make it. Yesterday I still had a temperature, but now I'm OK and I think it will pass. Then I'm sure I'll never catch cold again in my life.

Apparently they have stockings and clogs in the storeroom, but they're not giving them out. I don't know what they're waiting for.

*

The buildings were only recently finished and they've not dried out yet. Water drips from the ceiling, so every evening, our coverings and straw mattresses are completely wet. It might be better to sleep on the lower bunks – they're only two levels here – but there the moisture seeps in from below. There's hoar frost on the walls and they never light the stove. We're allocated two buckets of coal a day, but the guards steal half of it while we're at work. As of yet we have not been able to wash, only a bit in secret in the factory, at the water pipe in the lavatory. But Šára will slap you for that. The *Waschraum* is four buildings along from where we live; at the moment the water there is frozen.

We don't even undress at night; we sleep three to a bunk, as there are not enough straw mattresses. It's dreadful here. Unless a miracle occurs, we won't survive this. Maybe the end will be here soon. Supposedly they're in Bautzen already, for real this time; one of the foremen said so.

*

Shocking as it seems, Šára has taken pity on us. He admitted it's not possible to live in this damp. It's not that he actually cares about us, but he realized that we would all fall ill and what would the factory do without us? We're a trained workforce and many of the specialists have already gone off to the front. It was for the factory's sake that they moved us into a better building. It's also freezing cold in here, but at least the ceilings aren't dripping wet (at least not as much).

*

There's running water in the washroom now, but it's not possible to wash there; all the windows are broken. We stole buckets from the factory and wash ourselves in the buildings. Of course, Šára found out and at roll-call he explicitly forbade us from doing it. He or the overseers come round each morning to check. We wash at night; it's the safest way.

It's 29 January.

They distributed the stockings and clogs. We were lucky; Mum and I got both. There weren't enough for everyone; some people will have to go barefoot all winter. There are more in the storeroom, but apparently they're not giving them out.

I finally got out of polishing. They put me on the ground floor, in assembly. It's men's work, horribly hard. We're assembling enormous wings, standing on scaffolding to do it. My fingers are shot through from riveting; I can't seem to learn how to do it. I'm afraid the *Salmeister* in charge of us will complain to Šára. He's a real swine; even the specialists are afraid of him. Some of the rivet guns are so heavy that I can't even lift them.

We work from one in the afternoon till one in the morning. Wake-up call is at nine – supposed to be ten, but the guards are always in a hurry. At half eleven we leave the building; at half past twelve we have to be in the factory lined up for roll-call. Šára is always in a desperate hurry and waits on the steps with a strap in hand.

We used to save our bread and eat it before roll-call, but Šára won't permit it. He says we have to finish eating before we leave. We eat secretly at work, because it's impossible to hold out till evening on an empty stomach. Dinner is at seven p.m. The breaks are horribly short. By the time they distribute 1,000 portions the last people don't even have enough time to drink the water down (that's all it is by now).

The portions are awfully unequal, but that's the guards' fault for not stirring the cauldron at all. As if it were so much work. This way some people get a plate of water skimmed off the top and others get all the solid bits. Of course that's only for the guards' favourites. For ordinary mortals like me there's only ever water. It's the same with the bread, which we get at the same time as the soup. Šára walks around as they give it out and keeps order with his strap. If only he'd use it as they divided up the portions; that's where it's needed. But he and the guards are thick as thieves, otherwise they wouldn't be so mean to us. Of course – he's got no need to be fair.

*

My favourite part of the whole day is the time after we come back to the work hall. The specialists aren't yet back from dinner and the lights are out. Šára sends us back to work pointlessly early. I always climb up to the top of the scaffolding, to have a few minutes alone. It's the one moment of the whole day when I don't see other people. I remember . . . Dad and I promised we'd always think of each other at seven o'clock in the evening.

It's not possible in the confusion, crush and noise at mealtime. So this is half an hour later. Maybe Dad doesn't have time at seven o'clock either. Maybe he's asleep after the day shift; perhaps he's just starting work, or has a break at exactly the same time and is thinking of us.

~

I can rivet as well as any specialist now, but I don't really care whether we finish this plane or not. Although I would like to get the bonus. It's silly to get a reward for working for the Germans, but it wouldn't kill us. Once Mum and I got a package of soap powder. It lasted us almost two months. Yesterday I bought three spoonfuls of powder for two slices of bread. It's a hard price to pay, but there's no helping it. We're still wearing the same undergarments we got at Auschwitz. Mum got a bonus of 300 grams of bread. We ate it all at one sitting; for once we felt we had something in our stomachs. The *Salmeister* promises me every day that he'll put me forward, but it hasn't happened yet. By the time it's finally my turn, they won't be giving out bonuses. That's just my luck: I've never got anything in life, whether it's *Nachschub* – an extra portion – bonuses or anything else. Almost everyone has jumpers already, but I always get there too late.

Getting overalls without having to give up my stockings was a real piece of luck; I don't know where I got the courage and gall to do it. I simply took off my stockings, hid them under my coat and said I didn't have any. It was a big risk – what if Šára had come to check up? – but that's the only way to do things here. I have to learn a bit from the Poles; they know how such things work.

They gave out special *Zulags*, half a ration of bread and farmer's cheese for children. I got nothing, because I'm down as born in 1926. Also, when we worked until eight, children could go home at six, but not me. Once in my life I lied and all I've had from it are disadvantages. Of course it could also have turned out that, if I'd told the truth, they'd have split up me and Mum. They can keep their cheese, then.

*

There are air raids every day now, more and more often. The siren is endlessly going off and the *Voralarm* before the raids never stops. Yesterday there was a big air raid on Dresden. Shooting could be heard and at night, as we were coming back from work, the sky was completely crimson. Even today the glow is still visible.

For days, vehicles with refugees have been streaming constantly past along the road. It makes me feel so good; I'm always more cheerful on my way to work now. Three years ago it was us fleeing the air raids. They used to let us into the shelter here, but then thought better of it; they're afraid of not getting to safety in time themselves. So we always deliberately walked slowly. It's down to fate whether we perish or stay alive. Life matters so little to us; we have nothing to lose.

The one thing I'm afraid of is that only one of us will be killed. The moment the siren sounds, I'm up on the second floor by Mum's side. Then I couldn't care less whether we're hit or not.

So they won't let us into the shelter any more; we stay in the hall, all the women down on the ground floor. For now there have not been any air raids directly on Freiberg, but a number of times planes have circled over the factory. Today one plane was shot down; the specialists went mad with joy. They talked about it all day until by evening they'd turned one downed plane into three. Personally I am quite fond of air raids (and I think I'm not the only one). We don't have to work, I can spend a bit of time with Mum, and it's also terribly good fun to watch the specialists – sorry for the expression – wet themselves.

Kapteiner, my *Salmeister*, the one who shouts so much and drives us so hard, the one everyone quails before, is always the first out of the hall. A while back one of the specialists even broke his leg running to the shelter. Just wait till the real air raids start, every day, let them show the Germans what they can do – those idiots still believe they will win the war. With the very planes we're making here?!

I'm on day shift again. It's beautiful outside today. The sun is shining, the birds are singing; it's spring. And we're locked in this cold, grey factory. I've not done anything yet, I can't – I have to keep looking outside. I'm far from the window; all I can see is a bit of sky and the treetops. They're starting to bud. On the way from work we saw children playing marbles, spinning tops – in short, spring is here.

The specialists don't notice us much; there are so few of them here now, most have gone off to the front. We work completely independently – if only that Kapteiner didn't pay such close attention. Geňa – a Polish girl I work with – and I deliberately broke several light bulbs so we'd be able to go and get new ones. I don't feel like working today; it never interests me, but recently we're not even doing anything. Except we always have to be vigilant, so that Kapteiner or Šára don't catch us. I keep my hammer to hand; as soon as someone comes, I start riveting. Geňa, on the other hand, understands me. Always the same work. How long is there to go? Will this war never end?

*

Mum's legs got scalded when they were distributing coffee. Those awful Dutch girls – they always fight over the food like madwomen. Mum is in the infirmary. It's sad being alone here. Now I see how lucky we are to have stayed together.

*

Supposedly we won't be working in the factory any more. It will be liquidated; the front is getting close. We'll leave here – there are no trains; the specialists say we'll go on foot. That can't be possible, how far would we get? We'll see – not everything that's said has to be true. For now, work goes on as before.

This morning we started work as usual; the specialists didn't say anything at all and probably didn't even know. Suddenly the order came: 'Tools down.' Apparently we're not going back to the factory.

The last day we were at work, one woman disappeared. They threatened to cut off our hair if we didn't tell them what we knew. But would they really find her? They only found out twelve hours after it happened. Let them try to find her. Supposedly she fled with one of the specialists. By now she'll be who knows where.

They did frighten me a bit with the hair cutting. In Auschwitz I didn't really care, but now I wouldn't like it. The end is surely coming soon and it wouldn't be pleasant to go back to Prague with a shaved head. We won't escape it anyway; Šára has been in a bad mood recently and shaves people for every little thing. For example, he had one woman's hair cut off because he could see her hair underneath her kerchief (in the winter we were allowed to wear kerchiefs on the way to work). Another woman had made a ring out of a piece of wire, and a third had washed herself all over. All things that had been explicitly forbidden to us.

*

Šára left a few days ago. They say he went to arrange our departure for Flossenbürg. That's the concentration camp we belong to and that issued our prisoner numbers (*Häftlingsnummern*). My number is 54391. The number is imprinted on a metal disc and it is affixed to our clothing.

*

Šára has returned. He mocked us at roll-call, saying he'd heard some silly rumours about leaving. He knew nothing of it and forbade us to spread stories of this sort. So it is definitely true, otherwise he wouldn't be making so many excuses.

Mum decided to return from the infirmary. If we did go

[146]

anywhere, maybe the sick would have to remain behind or would all be shot. We can never know what might happen and the most important thing now is to stay together.

❧

There's no work here at all, but they keep at us to do it. Hoeing the beds, fixing the paths, digging up bushes and all sorts of pointless work. There are tools for maybe a hundred people and there are a thousand of us. Anyone who doesn't get a tool has to carry and break up rocks. It's still horribly cold outside – our buildings are located high up in the mountains – but Šára has resolved that we will work without coats. He and his *Aufsehers* are warm enough; they've got full stomachs.

It's a fortnight since we've worked in the factory. There isn't a single stone left lying anywhere in the whole camp, but we still have to move them. We carry them from one pile to another, just so it'll look as if we're doing something.

The situation with food is terrible. We don't even get a full litre of soup any more. It's unsalted; they've run out of salt. Only 170 grams of bread.

Mum looks awfully bad; she's skin and bones. Recently she's started having heart trouble. She's so weak she can barely stay on her feet. We're almost all that way; although I'm young, even my knees give way as I walk.

We were always hungry; hope sustained us. We were no longer living off that litre of water and slice of bread; you can't live off that. Now we live off the strength of our will. And we will survive! Some day, after all, the end must come.

Explosions can be heard. From one side they're attacking Dresden, from the other Chemnitz.

During the day there was a *Hochalarm* four times; apparently they're already at Dresden and in Chemnitz parachutists have gone in. A few women went to clean at the factory and brought back a newspaper. There are huge battles near Berlin, that's what it says in the newspaper – they must definitely already be in Berlin.

Often I sit by the window and look out at the white road in front of us. Soon, maybe tomorrow, the day after. That's how they'll come. God, when the first tanks arrive! They'll come to liberate us, we'll be free. And the end will soon come. After all, in the papers they almost admit that Berlin has fallen.

*

This morning they called Šára to the phone from roll-call. '*Vorbereiten zum Abmarsch! Schüssel und Decken mitnahmen!*' – 'Prepare to march! Bowls and blankets with you!' That was at three a.m.; at four we had roll-call and at five we set off.

I wanted to hide instead of forming up. Maybe in a pallet or one of the pits behind the building that we dug yesterday. They wouldn't waste time looking for us; Šára was terribly upset and in a hurry. The front must be very close. It might even reach Freiberg today. If only I knew for sure that it wouldn't last long – but what if it takes them a week to get here, or a fortnight? With a loaf of bread in hand I wouldn't have hesitated, but it would be hard to hold out a fortnight without any food at all.

I might just have stayed anyway, but Mum started having second thoughts. And kept having them until it was too late.

They split us into groups of five, counted us and off we went. At a clip. We'd always walked quickly on our way to work, but nowhere near like today.

Along the way and at the train station were refugees, one after the other, carrying bundles. The *Aufsehers* were taking their luggage with them. Šára had his wife along. They're all fleeing, the whole town has taken to its feet. They've only just realized? It's taken them a while to see the light. It's not the Americans they're fleeing; they're dreadfully afraid of the Russians. But they won't get away from them all the same.

They loaded us into open coal wagons, sixty to eighty persons in each. At eight o'clock the train left the station.

I'll never see Freibcrg again. I won't miss it, although it saddens me that I won't see the troops come. Maybe they're there already, coming down the road I looked at so longingly. Why didn't I hide, in the end?

⌒

We are crossing the Sudetenland. From the *Aufsehers*' conversation (there are two in cach wagon) we caught somcthing about Bavaria. Flossenbürg.

It's starting to get dark. They've not let us out of the wagons all day and have given us nothing to eat.

So, we're going to Flossenbürg. I didn't think I'd see the inside of another concentration camp. This morning I was in a good mood as I watched the Germans flee, but Flossenbürg!? We kept thinking that once danger threatened, they'd flee and stop worrying about us. And now this. In the end they'll just bump off all of us and it'll be over.

I can't even believe this will ever end. The war has lasted so long already. It was always 'in the autumn, in the autumn' and now it's almost summer and still nothing. The day before yesterday, even yesterday we were making plans, imagining them coming to liberate us, and now we're off to another concentration camp. They'll always have enough time for us.

We crossed through Most and are travelling on towards Chomutov. Everything here is all smashed up and the alarm just sounded. One railway worker, a Czech, shouted at us that they'd be here in two days. Within a week, he said, it'll all be over. If only he were right.

Now we're going the other direction again. Maybe the train's being shunted aside. No, it's returning back along the same route. Why? I can't worry about it now; we've got to lie down and get some sleep. In the morning we'll see where we are.

*

We didn't sleep, just dozed a bit sitting up. The fog is lifting and the sun is starting to come out. Please let it be nice out. The whole night beneath the open sky, covered only by a thin blanket. Will I ever get warm again? I feel like I won't.

Daybreak. We recognize places from yesterday. We're standing on the tracks outside Most. In front of us are rows of buildings, barbed wire. A concentration camp. Maybe they'll leave us here. We probably won't get to Flossenbürg now. They sent us back from Chomutov; apparently we can't go any further because of the front. There are people, men walking in front of the buildings. Maybe Dad's there. If only they'd unload us here, on the ground, let us sleep, even without blankets, just so we'd have a roof over our heads.

*

They have sent us on to a dead-end siding. It's been five days. We probably won't get out of the wagons till the war's over. All day, trains carrying wounded soldiers pass by. Twenty-four hours later they go back in the direction they came from. The front is on all sides; they don't even sound sirens for the air raids. There are constantly planes overhead. They shoot at them without interruption; the anti-aircraft fire bursts right over our heads. The first day we were a bit afraid, but now it doesn't bother us at all. A bomb could fall here, but I don't think about it. I believe nothing will happen to us. And if it does, at least we won't know about it. We won't be freezing and hungry any more.

The camp is named Triebschitz. We get food from there. A slice of bread and a half-litre of coffee. We drink half of it and use the rest to wash. In doing so we're cheating our bodies of a bit of liquid that they're yearning for, but we don't want to get lice. Each morning, even if it's cold, we strip and at least air out our undergarments and clothes. We've swept out the coal dust and we each have our own place. We had to get things organized; who knows how long we'll be on this train.

During the day it's bearable, but the nights can drive you mad. We've figured out there's only one way for everyone to lie down. We line up like sardines, starting the process before dusk, so we can get ready while it's still light. We all lie on our right side and if anyone turns over – which we've forbidden ourselves to do – the whole car has to do the same at precisely that moment.

Three of my toes have got frostbite – one so badly that I can't get it into my clog. We're lucky; the weather is relatively good, even though there are frosts at night, since it's only April.

*

I'm afraid of the nights; they are the worst ordeal. If only these women could be more understanding of each other. Each thinks only of herself and is indifferent to everyone else. Egoists, self-ish people. As long as she can sleep, everyone else can be up. Each thinks she's got the worst place and blames the others for having more space and for tormenting her. She gets up and in doing so wakes up the whole wagon. All the evening's counting and measuring was in vain; we won't be able to lie back down before morning again.

The *Posten*, our sentry, came twice, there was so much noise here. I thought it was only us, but when it gets dark you can hear arguments from all the wagons. It's probably also the hunger that makes us all so nervous.

Now it's even worse for me – someone is constantly stepping on my foot and the frostbite hurts horribly. They stepped on a blister on my big toe, broke it and it bled. I wrapped it in the old bandage from Mum's scalding, which is healing already – even here, in this filth!

This will be our sixth night in the train, a week in Trieb-schitz. I can't take it any longer. Every evening I think about it; tonight I might just do it. I'll jump under a passing train and commit suicide. I can't stand even one more night like this. But what if it is the end, what if this is the last time? I'll try it once more.

*

They've added two transports to ours. Greek women and Polish men. They're in terrible shape, much worse than us. They said they've not eaten for a week and have epidemic typhus. At night you can hear the wailing from there; they're calling out for water. They have a much worse Šára and *Aufsehers* than we do. They treat them horribly. We can't meet them; we only saw them when they went to the camp for food. They can't even walk, they just stagger. The men have striped clothes and look even worse than the women. My God, maybe Dad looks like that!

In the morning a men's transport from Buchenwald went by. They shouted at us. There were Poles, Hungarians, Slovaks and Czechs, but no one from Terezín. The way they looked! In comparison we're fat and beautifully dressed. They probably look so awful because they haven't been shaved. But all the same, they've gone through a lot. They were packed in even tighter than we are; they couldn't even all sit down and had to stand up so they'd fit.

We looked for Dad among them, but we probably wouldn't even recognize him. What can be left of a person – how can they treat someone that way?! I don't really even believe that Dad's still alive. He wouldn't survive it. And still there's no end.

*

Overnight there was a big air raid on Chomutov and Most. It looked like the end for us, but miraculously no bombs fell here. The *Aufsehers* and *Postens* fled, but we weren't allowed to leave the wagon. We were just as happy not to have to get up and we slept on peacefully. I only crawled out to look at the Stalin candles, which lit up the whole sky. Then I had to remain sitting till morning; I couldn't fit back in.

It was a huge air raid, but there was no siren at all; the front is certainly only a couple of kilometres from here. Maybe we'll live to be liberated after all.

During the air raid at night, a Slovak woman gave birth. In the dark, by the weak light of a torch that the *Posten* shone beneath the covers. For now the mother and child are both healthy. The fuss people would have made over a newborn at home – and here they simply wrapped him in a dirty, coal-smeared blanket. It's the second baby; the first was born the night before we left Freiberg.

~

The *Postens*, *Aufsehers* and Šára are awfully worked up. The Americans are already in Chomutov. We're travelling at great speed towards Most. They're shipping us with them as they themselves flee the advancing front. It's the second time it's come so close to us and once again we're going to miss out.

It's been raining more and more heavily all afternoon. The covers we're wrapped in are soaked through and sagging towards the ground. Soon it will be evening. We're travelling at great speed. If only it would stop pouring; we can't make it through the night like this in wet blankets. Perhaps they'll offload us somewhere for the night, maybe into a barn of some sort, if only to have a roof over our heads.

We're passing through a small village. Children are playing in front of the houses. They look at us, eyes agog, wave, those over there are shouting something. '*Nazdar!*' – 'Hello!' It's in Czech – they're Czech children. We're home, in Bohemia. The adults join in, the '*Nazdar!*' swells. My God, how beautiful it is to hear Czech again. What a difference between these Czech kids, the way they greet us, and those German brats who threw stones at us as we walked to work.

We pass a forest: a hare flees, a squirrel jumps through the trees. Nature is so beautiful. And the forest smells different from in Germany. A Czech forest. To be that hare, or that squirrel. Living free, breathing free. How happy those animals are. And where are we off to? Has Šára found a way to get us to Flossenbürg? Then this is the last forest I will see. The last bit of freedom. Tomorrow I might not even be alive. Is there a gas chamber in Flossenbürg? Oh, to jump from the train, hide in the forest, escape.

We stopped for a moment at a Czech train station. People run up to the train, throwing bread and rolls at us. My God, they are nice. They're all speaking Czech to us, saying it will soon be over.

Then we move onwards. It's pouring non-stop, but I don't even feel it. I don't care. My blanket has slipped off, people are treading on it underfoot, but I'm not bothered. One woman shares with us the bread that she got. We've not eaten since morning, I'm tremendously hungry, but I can't eat the bread. I clutch it to my chest; I don't feel the cold, rain or even the tears running down my face. I can't eat. It's bread from Czech people, our bread – we're home, in the Czech lands!

Two women have jumped out of our car. The *Posten* pretended not to see; the sentries don't care any more. I would like to escape, but it's harder with two. What if something happens to one of you as you're jumping; what if they catch one? If Mum were strong enough . . . but in the state she's in now, she couldn't escape. What if she ended up lying somewhere along the way? I won't jump; I'll leave it up to fate. There's no sign of life here. I have no idea where we are.

*

We're at the station in Horní Bříza. It's about midnight. It hasn't stopped pouring. The railway workers are shouting that in the morning we'll get covered cars. Morning – at least six hours to go. My frostbite is starting to burn and my neck hurts from the weight of my waterlogged blanket. Six more hours. The rain does not stop.

They transferred us into covered cattle cars. Now let it pour outside, at least we've got a roof. If only there were dry blankets – we'll never warm up this way.

*

The blankets have almost dried out; it doesn't feel cold any more. They've uncoupled us from that other transport. It's better that way; there were lots of sick people there and all we need is to catch an infection.

*

We left Horní Bříza early in the morning; we're probably headed for Plzeň. Šára knows that two women escaped, but he doesn't seem at all upset by it. We're probably not his concern any more.

By noon the train reached Plzeň. It stopped behind the train station, by a forest. Immediately loads of people converged on us with food. I don't understand where they got it all so quickly. It's Sunday; they must have already been baking. They're carrying full baskets and hampers full of bread, pastries, fruit. Except they're giving them all to Šára, who tells them he'll distribute it all to us. That I want to see.

For a bit they left our car open – there are a couple of women from Plzeň among us and they let people know, so we tossed out a few notes. We call out to the people to give the food to us themselves or make sure they're there when it's distributed. Šára will certainly keep it all for himself and his *Aufsehers*.

All the people here are so nice. All day they brought us food and made us soup. From morning till evening they brought it out here from the town. We each got a full bowl of real Czech potato soup. After two days, something hot to eat. They gave it out themselves – Šára was beside himself but couldn't do anything. He can't get away with as much as he used to.

We heard his conversation with the stationmaster, who was trying to convince him to leave us here. They would take care of us, he said, food, everything. He advised Šára not to travel onwards with us – apparently we won't get anywhere. But Šára wouldn't hear of it. He wants to leave here at any cost. He feels the end coming and is afraid to be among Czechs. He asked which direction it was to Bavaria. The stationmaster claims he can't get there, but Šára is beyond persuasion.

⌀

We're in a dead-end siding again. No sign of life here at all. We have no idea where we are. We think it might be near Domažlice. Šára is trying to get something to eat, but can't find anything anywhere. He's got no supplies, not even for his *Aufsehers*. Today they're eating all the pastries they didn't give us yesterday. Why didn't Šára stay in Plzeň? We'd have had food supplied; here we'll die of hunger.

We can't go any further. They turned us back at one station. It's awfully strange here, so dead. We are evidently in the war zone.

Yesterday they gave us no food at all, today they made tea on a campfire and sweetened it. Šára still has a bit of sugar. We don't even leave the carriages when they allow us to. It takes too much energy to clamber down. We can't even stand on our feet any more.

*

They gave each of us two spoonfuls of sugar. You wouldn't believe what it did for us. Instantly it set us aright. Mum and I went for a walk in front of the cars. We got a cup of water for washing. We're horribly dirty. Did we once wash ourselves in Triebschitz in a quarter-litre of coffee?

*

Šára scrounged some potatoes from somewhere with his own hands. They cooked them in buckets over a fire. Each of us got two. If we don't leave here soon, we'll perish. How long can we survive without food?

We're in Klatovy. Once again people come from all sides with food, but Šára won't let them close. There's a stream nearby; we're allowed to go and wash ourselves.

[158]

I tossed my jumper out of the window; there were lice in it. I'll be cold, but that's easier to endure than lice. Something's always biting me and I end up thinking about it constantly. We were so afraid of them that in Freiberg we tried hard to keep clean. Once they're here, we'll never get rid of them.

Mum is cross with me; she says I'm too highly strung, lice won't kill me and it's far worse that we've got no food. That's true, but the lice bother me more than the food does. It makes me miserable.

People would be happy to help us; why won't Šára let them? One girl, a mixed-race, has parents here in Klatovy. At night they called her name. She could have escaped, but is seriously ill. She'd been in the camp infirmary since Christmas. It's horrible, for her and her parents. So close to home, without food, without help.

*

They've moved us one station further on. The mother of the girl has been standing outside the train since morning. She was asking Šára and the *Aufsehers* to take her off the train and leave her here; even the block warden would have permitted it, since she's so sick. But Šára wouldn't allow it and wouldn't even let the woman come over.

The *Aufsehers* go into the town to beg for food. They return with full rucksacks and baskets, even bringing several jugs of milk, fruit, but it all disappears into the carriages with the *Aufsehers* and Šára. If only we could give people a sign. They certainly don't have food to waste – they're giving the best they have and Šára is scoffing all of it.

Tonight I'll escape. I'll definitely scarper – I've been planning it for a couple of days. The people here will certainly help us.

Šára changed his mind and let them come to the train. Even the mother of that girl. They made us white coffee and bread to go with it. A huge slice for each of us and pastries for the infirmary. What bread that was! The best pastry in the world couldn't taste better. And the coffee! Milky and sweet. The way a Czech kitchen smelled. It was high time they gave us something to eat. Aside from those two potatoes, half a mug of tea and two spoons of sugar we hadn't eaten in four days. That morning Mum fainted twice from weakness. In a little while they'll let us out of the cars; I'll look around outside and tonight, without fail, I'll leg it.

*

I still have to think it through. There's a watch posted all along the train. I looked to see if it would be possible to lie down under the train. But there are locomotives at both ends of the train and I don't know which direction we're going. There's still one option left. If they leave the windows open at night (the doors are locked from outside the whole time), we can jump. The people I've had the opportunity to speak with have warned us off this. There are apparently still constant searches. They can get us food, but where will we hide? We can't ask people to hide us and bring misfortune on themselves.

If I could be sure the end was near, then we'd hold out some-how. We'd sleep in the forests, in haystacks . . . after all, we're used to worse. However, how long could we live like that? At some point they'd certainly catch us. Mum still doesn't want to flee; she's afraid she's too weak. I don't want to try to talk her round. I'm just waiting on her word. If she says it, then I'll run for it with no further hesitations.

I'm waiting, maybe she'll say yes.

*

I stood by the window long into the night and looked out. Our place is right below the window, so I wasn't disturbing anyone. Around eleven we left Klatovy. We were going quite slowly, so it would have been perfect for jumping. But Mum was silent.

I suppose we can't go any further. The stationmaster in Plzeň was telling the truth that we wouldn't get any further than Horažd'ovice.

*

Hello, how did these people know we'd be coming this way? All of them are carrying loaves of bread under their arms. A railway worker threw Mum his own snack. Another asks if we're all Czechs. He passed us a loaf of bread and another one through the next window. 'Berlin has fallen. It'll be over within two days . . .' but then Šára ran up and hammered on the windows angrily with his gun.

It's dark in here, but at least he didn't see them passing us the bread. We divided it up; everyone got a slice. We hadn't eaten since yesterday; Šára said it wasn't necessary since we'd got food off people.

*

We rode onwards. Where to? After all, the track to České Budějovice is blocked.

We asked and called out for them to open the windows; it was suffocating in here. The *Posten* took pity on us and opened one, at least. A military train was standing opposite; they gave us a can of bean soup. We divided it up and each got a spoonful. At any rate, something warm for our stomachs. They would have given us more – they'd had some slices of bread ready – but Šára frightened them off by running over and banging on the window again. Only a small crack stayed open. The soldiers made a few remarks about inhuman behaviour. Maybe they're not all that evil; they're just afraid of one another, and mostly of the SS.

*

All the trains are going back towards Horažd'ovice but Šára apparently doesn't intend to. He always has to have his way and is intent on it this time too. He'll go where he wants to.

We asked one railway worker whether he knows where we're going. 'Mauthausen, probably.' Probably? No, people don't say things like that lightly. Ten women jumped out of our car overnight. The Germans shot at them, but I don't think anything happened to any of them. Probably even the *Postens* didn't want to hit them. They don't care what happens to us; one of them has even disappeared.

Still, I wouldn't try anything here. If I wouldn't escape in Bohemia, should I risk it here in České Budějovice, which is full of Germans?

Now it's too late. I'll stay and hold out till the end. If I'm fated to die, so be it. Let God's will be done.

*

They've figured out that there are ten fewer of us. They threatened to punish us, but what else can happen to us? Is there anything worse than Mauthausen?

*

'Water, drink, only a drop, wet our lips. *Wasser, bitte, trinken!*'
They don't hear, they don't want to hear. We don't feel hunger
any more – we're used to going without food, but thirst, unbridled
thirst, tortures us.

*

Through the cracks rays of sunlight filter in. You can see a bit
of the sky, here and there a tree trunk or treetop. That must be
a forest. Oh, looking at a forest makes me saddest of all. I love
them so. Dad loved them too. The grass over there is rippling.
God, the world is so beautiful.

Šára won after all. So, what of all those pronouncements that
we'd never get anywhere? How many times did they say the end
was coming? Our sixteen-day journey is at an end. The cars are
open, and on the wall opposite is written in large, black letters:
'MAUTHAUSEN'.

*

I saw myself in the window glass. And frightened myself. How
can a person change so much in sixteen days? We're all altered
beyond recognition. Sunken cheeks, bulging eyes. Who cares?
It's trivial to notice such details – here, at Mauthausen.

They lead, or rather force, us along the road through the town. People look out of the windows, curious children run out into our path. How many transports have gone down this road? How many breaths, tears, beads of sweat and blood have soaked into its dust?

Yesterday at this time we were still in Bohemia. I saw the Czech land, I heard the Czech language. I will no longer see or hear either. And no one will ever find out that we perished here in Mauthausen.

*

I can't go on. I can't move any further. I'll lie down here – let them shoot me. The blanket is so heavy; I can't even hold my bowl. If they'd only let us rest a moment, an instant, just to catch our breath. Or allow us a drink. If we'd been allowed to drink from the pump at the train station, we'd be able to go on. The road climbs a hill, ever steeper. They drive us on at a mad pace. A drop of water, a single swallow . . . I can't go on.

The road narrows to a trail. We must be there already. Just a bit further. I gather my last strength. I must make it. There – what is it? A spring, water flowing down a slope. Maybe it's a stream, rainwater, maybe overflow from the canal. No point thinking about it – quickly, Šára is in front and the *Aufseher* has her back turned. One more gulp, how it cools and refreshes . . .

A stone wall comes into view, towers, the camp gates. Does anyone return from here alive?

*

We stopped so they could count us. Our last minutes in the free air. In a couple of minutes, five, maybe ten, those tremendous gates will close behind us and then . . .?

The setting sun leans into our backs and the fresh green grass ripples in a light breeze. A beetle crosses the path and a bit further along a butterfly settles on a flower. I never knew how much I loved this world. How much of it have I experienced? Fifteen years; of those, three and a half in the camp. And now, when I've made so many plans, now, when life can really begin . . .

*

We're off. The gate is wide open and waiting. Now they'll split me and Mum up. Maybe we're going right into the gas. 'Mum, thank you for everything and if you ever see Dad again and I don't, thank him for me. For everything.' One more kiss and the gates swallowed us up. 'God, do not abandon us . . .'

On one side, a stone wall with barbed wire; opposite, an even larger stone building. We sit on the ground, while among us run the '*Schupo*', the state police, in yellow uniforms. Šára has turned us over to the local authorities.

We get coffee, a full bowl, and can go for seconds, as much as we want. I pour a third portion into myself; where's it all going? I can only feel my slightly moist tongue, but inside nothing, dusty, dry. Maybe I don't have anything inside any more. The *Schupo* give out cigarettes, chocolate, talk with us, calm us down, comfort us. Aren't we going to be gassed? Won't we be put to work? Aren't they going to cut our hair off again? Will we stay together? No, nothing will happen to us, there's no one to work for. The front will be here within a week.

Why the ironic answer to that girl who was looking for her sister: '"Sister" does not exist; here you are things.' Why did they beat back the prisoners so cruelly when we went by the buildings? I don't want their chocolate; anyway it's stolen from the packages for prisoners. They can keep their cigarettes. There's nothing true in what they're saying. They're lying, playing with our fears, having fun at our expense. I don't believe them.

*

They line us up in pairs. We get coffee again and – bread! Really, bread, a whole 300-gram ration and 20 grams of margarine. Bread, my God, to bite into it again after sixteen days, a whole 300 grams will belong to me alone; I can eat it all at one sitting. I can already feel how my jaws will break up and grind the pieces, the crumbs melting on my tongue, the bitter taste of ration loaf. We're moving up, in a few minutes, a few seconds I'll be holding it in my hands. Bread, a whole chunk of bread!

I got a beautiful ration, the heel. Then they took us along the other side behind the building. The *Schupo* started to shout, beat us with cat-o'-nine-tails: the ones in front pushed us back and those in the rear wouldn't let us out. Straps, insults, blows. Confusion. They threw me on the ground, poured out my coffee and snatched my bread. Mum stayed at the back. Afraid of losing her, I call out, she sees me, pushes forward; they knock her down and the bread vanishes in the scrum.

The *Schupo* calmed down; we pick ourselves off the ground. The Polish women are fighting; the Hungarians are arguing;

puddles of coffee, shards. Mum made her way to me, giving up our bundle of things (a piece of soap, shirts, a washcloth, a bit of jacket lining, a handkerchief, some washing powder – a bonus from Freiberg – a spoon, a cup, my pencil, a piece of paper). What of it? We won't need anything any more, we're in Mauthausen and that's the end. The end of the war might not be far off, but even if it's only a week away, our end will come first.

We go back to our former place to wait for our baths – not for the gas . . .? I split my margarine – the one thing left in my hand – with Mum.

*

In fact, it was not gas and they let us keep our hair. Just a bath, lovely hot water and plenty of time to wash.

How long would I need to wash off all this filth? It doesn't matter; the worst is down the drain, and mainly it's just having that feeling of cleanliness again. We took off our old clothes; the only things we're allowed to keep are the clogs.

They distribute underwear. Men's boxers and undershirts. That's all we get, but despite that they are completely new shirts, never worn. Finally we're rid of the lice. And then – they didn't gas us, didn't cut our hair off, clean underclothes and decent behaviour. Have we finally made it?

*

Through the main gate, the mud and up the stairs, and we're here. Our teeth chatter, but that's nothing, they're sorting us out into buildings. They shove us on to overfilled bunks, three, four on each. Some people are up. The Poles, Hungarians, Greeks, a few Czechs. The rest sleep on uninterrupted. Or are they corpses? You can't tell the living from the dead: it's dark, the lights aren't on. We'll see in the morning. I suspect we're in the infirmary.

At the doorway they shoved a bowl of soup at each of us. 'Do you want more?' they ask. We do not understand. We grope at the contents: a bowl full to the brim, its bottom hot. A pleasing smell and warm steam wafts to our noses. I sip as I walk. And the taste so well known from Auschwitz. At the time I didn't like it, but today it's superb.

Someone tugs at my sleeve, shoves her portion at me. Thank you, and a second serving vanishes instantly into my innards. My cheeks flush, a pleasant warmth runs through my body, my intestines start to work, my legs are steadier and I can stand more firmly on them. I no longer regret my lost bread; I have a full stomach and thus good cheer. No one is hounding us, shouting at us; what can it mean?

A group of men arrives: Czechs bringing us food, searching for blankets for us, places for us to sleep. They help us on to the bunks, promise to help, tomorrow they'll come again.

*

No roll-call, nothing. We can do what we want. Empty tins of food roll about on the bunks, chocolate wrappers, boxes and papers with the Red Cross's label. I truly do not understand. The end? But, God, now I can finally look round at where we are. An infirmary, without a doubt, but the state of it! Last night we were tired and couldn't have cared less. We were overjoyed at the clean shirts and covers. But at night everything looks different from during the day. The shirts are clean, true, but horribly lice-infested. The covers kept us nicely warm and thus

I don't throw mine off, although all night I knew what that repulsive smell was. An infirmary where the only illnesses are typhus and diarrhoea. What else could blankets look like that have done duty here for years on end . . .

Stench, filth, lice, the sick and the dead. Men or women? The elderly? Children? It's day already, but I was wrong to think I'd be able to tell in the morning. They don't move. Their breath, the only sign of life, is so feeble that I can hardly even make it out on the person in the neighbouring bed. Some people are still standing, or rather wobbling on their feet. Apathetic, speaking with no one, their eyes are cloudy, expressionless. Sunken cheeks, limbs and body parts, bared with cracks in dirty lines, bones visible beneath ashy grey, yellowed skin bitten by lice and covered in boils from the dirt, malnutrition and vitamin deficiencies.

You want to start talking to them, catch their attention, make them happy, say, perhaps, that it's over already (after all, maybe now it really is), but something stops you, you're almost afraid of them – you feel that before your eyes, Death herself is walking past. (That's how she must look.) You try it with a smile, but no luck, their sight is fixed on an indefinite point; without noticing you they grasp and support themselves on the headboard, walking – no, floating past the bunks. From their spot to the latrine and back.

You want to entice a smile on to these people's faces? Fool! Weeks, maybe months without food and drink. Yes, that's the last system. Physical and spiritual torture became commonplace and then – the mortality rate wasn't high enough – here in the *Krankenlager*, the sickbed, at the whim of lice and the typhus bacilli, what have these – people? – gone through?

Yes, they were once people. Healthy, strong, with their own will and thoughts, with feelings, interests and love. Love for life, for good things, for beauty, with faith in a better tomorrow. What's left are phantoms, bodies, skeletons without souls.

*

The Czechs are here again, bringing several spoons as promised, pieces of bread. They have a bit of time with us, looking for and asking after people they know. We talk about Prague, Brno, our homes, life in the camps, news from the front. They ask and answer . . . 'Are there any Jews here?' 'There were, ten days ago.' 'Not any more? What happened to them?'

They don't want to give an answer to these questions. They skip over them silently, or with some excuse, or simply, 'Don't ask.' Fine, that's enough, we know everything. 'And one more thing.' It seeps out of them slowly, but it's out. What was done here recently, especially with the Jews, simply can't be told. Even our transport was destined for the gas chambers! They gassed the last thousand on Wednesday, then the Red Cross stepped in. Today is Monday. So we came four days too late. If not for that attempt to get to Flossenbürg . . . it was the one thing that saved us. Luck? Coincidence? Fate?

'Dishes for dinner!' We have none; we gave ours back yesterday. There are tins and bowls rolling about under the bunks. The sick must have used them as washbowls or perhaps for other purposes. No matter; after all, in the train we too ate and washed from the same vessel, they'll do.

*

A figure sits motionless on an overturned box by the stove. I've been watching her since morning and I think she had been sitting here last night when we arrived. A little while ago someone threw a blanket over her. So that's it – but why doesn't anyone take her away?! Children scurry past, a bit further away an infant cries. It's the one that was born in the car on the way from the train up to the camp.

*

They brought a pile of clothes to the front of the building; they're ours, supposedly disinfected. We can't find our own, so once again we take someone else's. We are not allowed back in the building. We got our dinner: dried vegetables cooked in water. They write us down in the card ledger, for the third time or so today.

*

We walk for about a half-hour. The camp is a good way behind us. Steps, an awful lot of steps. There's one quarry after another, here and there we meet prisoners. We're being moved, to a women's camp, they say. And what if it's to be gassed? The ones up there said that's over with, but who believes the Germans? So, the Czechs confirmed it? They just didn't want to frighten us. 'Mum, we're going to be gassed, you'll see.' 'So let's go, then, what am I supposed to do?'

That's an answer for you! I know we're powerless, but can I really just not care? To perish now, when the end might come any day, any hour? Gas! Gas? No, we're being moved to a women's camp.

*

It wasn't the gas chambers, or a women's camp. A huge wooden shack in the forest with a sign: 'Wienergraben'. A barbed-wire

[171]

fence round it, a row of taps with running water, underneath them a trough and a latrine next to it. Inside, pallets and mud. Russian women live here; the guards are Gypsies.

We lie four to a pallet crammed into the aisle. There was a two-hour roll-call this morning; since then we've not been allowed to move or the Gypsy women are here immediately with cudgels and whips. The Russians are at work; they go to dig roads somewhere. We got nothing for supper, a scant quarter-litre of coffee for two persons for breakfast, a half-litre of soup for dinner.

<hr/>

1 May 1945

Second day in the Gypsy camp. Second day without bread, with a quarter-litre of coffee and the same amount of soup. Long morning roll-calls in the cold and mud. My clogs are so full of holes that I'm basically barefoot, with water running into them. Curses, blows.

*

It's three in the afternoon. We've still had nothing to eat. I can barely get Mum to roll-call in the morning and then off to the latrine. She lies down; it's all the same to her. I begged some potato peelings off the Russian women and cooked a soup from them. It made Mum sick; I put some grass I picked into it, and it must have been poisonous. The *Schupo* are giving out cigarettes. I wheedled three of them. Yesterday the Russian women were trading potatoes for them. They bring them from outside; they must be working near a field. Two potatoes for one cigarette.

Maybe they'll be trading them again today. Three cigarettes is six potatoes, they could save Mum. If only they'd come already; Mum's so ill. Maybe . . . I don't even want to finish the thought. They aren't accepting people in the clinic. I'm so helpless. Desperate.

*

So it's the first of May. The day we waited and hoped for. Rumbling can be heard in the distance, but that's probably the quarries. And to top it all those repulsive lice. Every time I check I find at least twenty of them. I've not washed since I got here. I don't have enough strength. I'm just glad I can still stand on my own two feet.

Outside the kettle is clanging; they've brought the soup. A quarter-litre per person. That's our First of May celebration. I don't believe anything any more. World, I bid thee farewell.

5 May 1945

Early morning. I sit behind the building by the campfire and wait to see if one of the Russian women throws away any potato peelings. They don't want to give them to us any more; they keep them and cook them for themselves. They've not been to work since Thursday and don't have any fresh supplies of potatoes. At the time they came back with much rejoicing, saying they didn't have to work any more because it would all be over. We celebrated with them – but as it turned out, prematurely.

Every night we hear the shooting; supposedly they're in Linz already, 27 km from here. If only it were true. The whole week we've only had a sixteenth of a loaf, twice, that's 70 grams. The Gypsies are worse than Germans. They beat us, cursing, threaten us with all-day roll-calls, and of the little bit of food we get, they steal half, if not all of it.

*

Mum is getting weaker day by day. A little while ago I led her outside into the fresh air and it made her so dizzy that she couldn't walk back. She was already weakened in Freiberg; the sixteen-day trip made things worse and now she's been here a week without food. I'm really frightened for her. I look dreadful myself, it's true, but at least I still feel strong; I can make it another month. I have to make it! I want to live, to return home. God, have mercy, give Mum enough strength so she too can see us liberated.

*

Late morning. Loads of Germans are here: the *Schupo*, *Postens*, *Aufsehers*. They are after civilian clothing to change into. The Gypsies are packing up; vehicles full of luggage pass through the forest. The explosions last night were very strong, several times they shook the building and now the Germans are starting to flee. Actually, individuals have been disappearing since Thursday. I'm starting to believe again.

*

Noon

The guard booth in front of the entrance is empty. The *Schupo* aren't promenading as usual in front of the building; the Gypsies are gone. Where have they gone? Half an hour ago they were still here. They even pushed me away roughly when I tried to take new clogs from out of the pile to replace my broken ones. (I still managed to steal a pair.)

What's happening?

They start to distribute soup. Today we'll get a bit to eat again: I have some boiled potato peelings, in salted water, even – one of the Russians gave me some salt.

What's happening? They've stopped giving out soup. Near the entrance everyone stands up, runs out, people hug one another. Why don't they stop playing around and give out the food? That's more important than anything else. Mum is ill, she's waiting for a bit of that water – after eating a little of her strength always returns.

People are gathering outside, the rejoicing reaches all the way to us. Some more *bonkes*, rumours like the ones the Russians came back with that time? I quickly finish my peelings and listen.

I can pick out individual voices now in the clamour. Am I hearing right? I put down my unfinished bowl and run outside. The voices grow, all of them blending into a single tone. 'Peace, peace, peace!!!' flies from mouth to mouth across the whole building. I stop in front of the gate. Everyone's gaze is fixed upwards; I turn my head in that direction. What is it I see? Am I dreaming? Can I really believe it, can it be true?

I'm not sleeping, I'm awake. I am standing behind the barbed wire of a Gypsy camp and up high, on the tower of Mauthausen – a white flag flutters! A flag of peace.

Mauthausen has capitulated, peace has come to us. 'PEACE,' I repeat to myself and every nerve in my body trembles beneath this word like a string. My legs break into a run all by themselves. Muddied, in my bare stockings just the way I'd run out, I arrive back at our space. Mum stands up – where has she found the strength all of a sudden? – I hang myself around her neck and, between kisses, I spill out, jubilantly, the word we've dreamed of for years. The word we indulged ourselves with in the most secret corner of our being and feared to pronounce aloud. That sacred word, which contains so many beautiful, unbelievable things: liberty, freedom. The end of tyranny, misery, slavery, hunger. Today I can pronounce it in public, without cringing, today it has come true.

The voices thrum and people repeat as if in a fevered ecstasy: PEACE, PEACE, PEACE . . . It seems as if everyone's singing with me. The woods, nature, the building is friendlier; I feel like dancing, whooping. We made it. We survived the war. PEACE IS HERE.

◦————

Night-time, 21 May 1945

16 days after liberation, 12 days after the end of the war.

In clean clothes, sewn by hand from SS bedcovers, with a full stomach, in a second-class local train. The final screech of the brakes and the loudspeaker announces up and down the platform: 'The train from Mauthausen is departing on track three!'

The platform of Wilson Station. The clock shows a quarter to two. I stand at the window and large, hot tears run down my cheeks. Tears of joy and happiness. Finally: Prague, the city we yearned for.

Finally home.

Children watch an outdoor performance at one of the homes set up for young Displaced Persons in Czechoslovakia after the war, 1945–7.

Interview with Helga Weiss

Neil Bermel spoke with Helga in her flat in Prague on 1 December 2011. The following is an edited version of their conversation, translated from the Czech. Additions and clarifications made by the translator and editor are in square brackets.

Could you tell us something about your parents: what their names were, what they did, what they were like before the war? From the diary we learn only that they were Mum and Dad . . .

My father's name was Otto Weiss; he was very educated, loved music, wrote poetry as well. He worked as a bank clerk. In the First World War, when he was eighteen, he was badly wounded in his right arm. My mother, Irena, born Fuchsová, trained as a dressmaker; she stayed home and ran the household. We weren't rich, but my parents created a home that was full of love. I had a happy childhood.

What was the fate of your friends, acquaintances, relatives?

In general things ended badly. Sadly . . . My father probably went to the gas chambers. But we never found out for sure. There's even a book, *The Terezín Memory Book*, where people's details are recorded in brief. There's always the date they were sent to Terezín, the date they were sent onwards and, if it's known, the concentration camp they were sent to. But for Dad the last mention is the date he left Terezín. That's the last trace of him.

Even with all those reports, daily attendances, and so forth . . .?

Later we searched everywhere, combed through all those papers, asked people who came back from various camps whether they'd seen him. There's no further trace. Probably he went straight off the train to the gas chambers. Dad was forty-six, but one reason might have been the fact that he wore glasses – that was a mark of the intelligentsia, and they got liquidated first – or he also had a scar on his arm, because he'd been badly wounded in the First World War. So there could have been two reasons: glasses and that scar.

They didn't need reasons, though, did they?

And so in all probability he went straight to the gas chambers.

And Ota?

I don't know anything further about Ota. After the war I visited his sister; he'd given me her address. She was in a mixed marriage and even had a child during the war. I went to see her after the war, but couldn't find him anywhere. Finally I found his name; it's written here in Prague. It's in the old Pinkas Synagogue, which is now a memorial. The walls are covered from top to bottom with the names of the eighty thousand people who perished. So I found him inscribed there.

And I think you've written about Francka that . . .

Francka didn't come back.

You've written that of the fifteen thousand children who passed through Terezín, about a hundred survived . . .

That's true. Of the ones who were sent on from Terezín, only a few were saved and they were mixed-race kids, the children of mixed marriages. It's interesting: I don't know why, but the mixed-race boys were sent onwards [to other camps], while the girls somehow managed to stay in Terezín, so some of them survived.

So of that whole group of yours that was there . . .?

Well, now there are only a few of us.

I'd like to ask you about how you lived in Terezín . . .

Terezín had been an ordinary town, a regimental town with lots of barracks. And around the barracks lived the normal civilian population. When the transports started in November 1941, the civilians were still living there. So at the beginning we just lived in the barracks. These were enormous dormitory barracks; sixty or a hundred people could live there. But the number of people kept increasing. Terezín was originally for about seven thousand inhabitants including the soldiers and all of a sudden there were about sixty thousand of us there. After a few months the civilian population had to move out, and then they divided us up and we lived everywhere, even in the civilians' homes. Of course, it wasn't as if we were allocated flats; they were just rooms and we lived the same way there. So each person had 1.80 square metres of space. And people filled up the barracks. Some then stayed in the barracks and others were sent into housing blocks, and later people lived in lofts and former shops and various warehouses – basically everywhere.

Is it true that some of the inhabitants felt themselves to be somewhat better than others?

Yes, of course, such castes did exist there to some extent. First there was the *Ältestenrat* [the Council of Elders]. That was our self-governing body. So they were the highest society, and yes – maybe I mentioned it somewhere – some of them came across as a bit arrogant. The first transport was 24 November [1941] and the second a few days later. And those were all male; they were called the AK, which was from the German word *Aufbaukommando*, construction squad. And they were the ones who went to get the ghetto ready. They were given certain benefits, and for a time they were even protected from further deportations. Because they said: 'We built all this' and 'We slept on the concrete.' By implication: 'You have something better to sleep on.' So that was the *Ältestenrat*, and the gradations went on down from there.

As far as accommodation goes, one of the best things that the *Ältestenrat* did was to try first of all to protect the children from the difficult conditions, to the extent that they could. So they identified suitable buildings from those in the vicinity and set up children's homes. There was a children's home; there was even a home for mothers with small children, newborns, because a few children were born there. That was the *Säuglingsheim*, from *Säugling*, baby. Then there was the *Kinderheim*, for younger children;

then two homes, one for boys and one for girls: *Knabenheim* and *Mädchenheim*. The *Mädchenheim* is the one where I lived. It was for girls from about ten to seventeen. And then there was the *Lehrlingsheim*, which was for adolescents. And that's where we were cared for by the *Betreuers*.

So is that why your father was so insistent on you moving to the girls' home?

Yes, of course, because things were better for us there. Conditions there were basically the same as for the adults. We had only 1.80 metres of living space, a bunk, but of course it was better and easier to be among children than to live with the elderly, where people were ill, they were nervous, there were various misunderstandings, people were dying and . . . Well, it was just better for the children to live separately.

Whenever you were summoned for deportation from Terezín, you immediately had to find a way to get the notice rescinded. How did that work?

Of course, the fear of being allocated to a transport was always with us, and everyone tried to avoid it. So it happened that when people found themselves in a transport, they tried to get themselves recalled from it. One excuse, for instance, was infectious diseases. The Germans were horribly afraid of people spreading infections. So if someone got, I don't know, scarlet fever or something, then at least for the moment that would protect him from deportation and his family along with him.

Later people also started to appeal to their bosses in various departments, arguing that their work was indispensable. And if the work truly was indispensable, then they would leave them there. For example, there was one German in Terezín named Kursavy, who oversaw a group of women agricultural labourers. And he did in fact protect them. Sometimes it would happen that, I don't know, the mother of one of the women would be in a transport and the daughter would volunteer to go with her mother, and he wouldn't give her permission. Because we didn't know what was coming, only that it would be something worse. But they really did know, and he didn't let them go. I think he even permitted her to save her mother. So that was one of those recalls.

But you felt that there was something going on in those other camps and that, at the least, it would be worse.

We knew it would be worse. But we had no idea even where the transports were going. We did know, to some extent, that concentration camps existed – they'd existed before the war, in Germany. But that we were being sent to other camps, that gas chambers existed, and death trains, where we'd . . . We had no idea of that at all.

At least that was the case while you were still at Terezín. Because later, at Auschwitz . . .

But even there we had no idea until the moment we got there.

But when you were at Birkenau, there you must have known, because the wardens were threatening you directly.

There we did know, because when we arrived, they just showed us the chimneys back there where we thought it was some sort of factory – and they told us straight off it was a crematorium. And there was dark humour: for example, 'The soot will fly up the chimney tomorrow and that's you done for.' So there we knew about the gas chambers, but we hadn't known until the moment we got there.

That constant threat of deportation from Terezín must have affected you in some way.

Of course it did. Some more highly placed people almost certainly knew what was coming. Because there were one, maybe two prisoners, Vrba and Lederer, who got out of Auschwitz, and they brought a message, a warning, with them. The message got to England, I think to Churchill, and to America. No one believed it. No one, nothing. Either they didn't believe it or wouldn't lift a finger. And I think the leaders in the ghetto who did know didn't tell us, because panic would have broken out.

Probably the only one who said he'd tell us and that it wouldn't happen here was Jakob Edelstein. The leaders had to pick up their orders at the German *Kommandatur*, a building in Terezín – today it's a bank – and beneath it was a bunker, which was the prison. Edelstein went to pick up some order or another, told them he was going to tell people and they never let him out. He stayed in that bunker and then left in a prisoners' transport. Actually it was a normal deportation train to which they added one special carriage with a notice saying that it was for prisoners. Immediately upon arrival those people were liquidated. It's known that they shot Edelstein's wife and son in front of him, and only then did they shoot him.

You described all this as a child. It must have looked to you like senseless confusion at the time, but there had to have been rigorous planning involved.

It did look like confusion on the surface, but it was an extremely well-thought-out operation. It had been thought through from beginning to end, starting with small decrees and escalating into that final liquidation.

What led you to start writing your diary?

Well, events were such that I started to write them down; I thought it would be important for them to be recorded.

And can you remember one specific impulse, an event of some sort?

Not at the beginning . . . Of course, I always followed the political situation. My father was quite active in politics, so people we knew used to meet at our house and debates went on – and I listened to all of it. I even remember when once they forgot to mention something to me and I was so insulted; why hadn't they told me? So I think I understood the situation well enough – in my own way, maybe, but I did understand it. And so I started to write things down.

Who were you writing for? Was it just for yourself?

I was writing only for myself, and I don't think that I had any special plans beyond that. Well, maybe I did, maybe I didn't; I don't know. But I drew as well. I drew for myself, although maybe I was also thinking – just a little bit, if I try today to follow my train of thought at the time and if I can put those thoughts in order – about the fact that this needed to be recorded. Mainly I was writing for myself, but perhaps there was just a little bit of that [idea] in there somewhere.

Were there many children who kept diaries?

Yes, I think there were a lot. In Terezín loads of children kept diaries; and not only children, adults as well, because people needed to come to terms with the situation and so they started to write. They wrote poems as well – people who had never done so before and wanted to take part in the cultural life [of the camp]. So there are a number of these diaries around.

Some of the events at the beginning of your account were originally described retrospectively, but eventually you move to a style of narration that is very immediate, describing things almost as if they were just happening. Where approximately in the notebooks does that retrospective stance end and this more immediate stance begin?

I used the past tense in the first few pages, where I'm describing the mobilization of 23 September 1938 and the occupation of 15 March 1939. Then there are eight more pages in the past and gradually I move over into the present. I changed these first pages into the present right after the war, when I was writing up my experiences from the other concentration camps. At the time I wanted the diary to form a cohesive whole – a testimony about those times. I did the same thing with my drawings: in Terezín I also painted an event that had occurred before our deportation ['List of Possessions', see page 32].

In the part you wrote upon returning to Prague, you continued to narrate events as if they were going on right now, as you were writing them down.

At the time I was already thinking about the fact that I had to write everything down chronologically, and I was writing just after the war, probably still in 1945, or at the latest 1946. And at the time I was still so vividly inside it all that I can say that it was as if I was writing it there and then. It was deliberate: I wrote it in the present tense, even though it was written afterwards.

And was that connected with the way you'd written earlier: that you'd always written that way, as things were happening?

Well, I followed on from where I'd left off [at fourteen]. And in the same manner. When I came back [from the camps], I was fifteen and a half. So it wasn't all that great an age difference, but I think that psychologically I was much further along at that point.

So would it make any sense to put it back into a past form of narration, or not?

No, I think it's more effective in the present. And when I wrote it, I lived through it all again. Even today, they invite those few of us who came back to visit various schools and gatherings to talk about ourselves. And I think it wrecks us; physically, of course, it wrecks us, but it wrecks us psychologically as well. Because I catch myself as I'm talking about it, and when I talk, I relive it; I'm still in it. So it's still the present, even though it's the past. And it's still just as vivid.

[188]

As you re-read your diary in preparing the manuscript for publica-
tion, did any absences surprise you? I mean things that were so
self-evident to you back then that it didn't even occur to you to
describe them?

I think I wrote down most of the main things. There were a
couple of things, maybe a few things I mentioned where I said
to myself later that this could have been a bit longer, so I sometimes added a word or term here or there. But basically I think
I'd written down all the main things. When I read it recently
after all these years, I even noticed some things in it that I'd
since forgotten about. Of course, I used Terezín slang in my
diary, which these days no one understands, and it needs some
explanation.

One very specific word from Terezín slang is šlojska.

The word *šlojska* comes from the German word *Schleuse*, which
means a sluice. When a transport of people came into Terezín
or as they were leaving, they had to be channelled through a
place – in other words, a sluice – where they would take various
things out of people's luggage that weren't supposed to be there.
That activity became a verb, *šlojzovat*, 'to sluice'. So it has two
meanings: either it's a noun, the sluice as a place, or a verb,
meaning 'to pilfer'. And in Terezín there was a huge difference
between stealing and 'sluicing'. You 'sluiced' from common
property, like when we were working in the fields, where we'd
'sluice' some vegetables, which was forbidden. But of course, if
I'd taken something that belonged to a particular person, from
his suitcase or his shelf, then that was stealing. There practically
wasn't any theft there; at least in our children's home, I can't

remember anything like that ever existing. And I think that it really didn't, but there was an awful lot of sluicing.

You also wrote about how you went to help out in the Schleuse.

I even have two pictures from it. One is in pencil, I think it was an arrival. And I have another picture called 'The "Sluice" in the Courtyard' [see colour inset]. People were channelled into various places for the sluice and that courtyard was one of them. Some of the people boarding were old and sick, and so services were provided. We even used to volunteer for this; we'd help the old people, we'd lead them, help with their luggage and so forth. So that was helping out in the *Schleuse*.

A few more specific points about Terezín: for example, daily attendance.

A roster was written out daily showing how many people were there. Every day the so-called *Zimmerälteste* [the room's elder] would make a report. He'd hand it in and it would get passed onwards. And these reports were brought daily to the German *Kommandatur*. So they would always have an overview and know whether anyone was missing. They constantly had to announce how many people were there today, how many had died. And the roster had to agree. Every day. And each day the so-called *Tages-befehl* would come back from the *Kommandatur*; those were the daily orders.

And roll-call, which happened more often in those other camps . . .

Terezín didn't have roll-calls, but Auschwitz and the other camps did, and there they would count us. Physically. It wasn't just writing something down, and I think it wasn't always just for the purpose of counting us, because that could have been done more quickly. At roll-calls we would stand there for hours. Hours in the cold, the rain, the snow – we always had to go outside somewhere and stand in groups of five as they counted us over and over. Constantly.

So it had a psychological purpose . . .

That too, or physically breaking us. You would stand there with no food, in the cold or the heat, no going to the loo. And they'd count us. So that was roll-call.

You also came into contact with people of various nationalities in the camps – Czechs, Poles, Germans . . .

In Terezín the Jews were primarily Czech, and later people from Germany, Holland, Denmark and Hungary were deported there as well. So we could encounter them, but by and large each national group stuck together. For instance, in our girls' home we were all Czechs. Then there was another home where the kids from Germany lived.

Could you explain some of the terms you used for people? For example, in Terezín I noticed Betreuer, Heimleiter, betreuerka . . .?

That's right. Because these were official matters, the language was German. And so all the announcements and orders that were brought each day from the *Kommandatur* were also in German. But of course we put these forms into Czech, because in correct

German it's *Betreuer/Betreuerin*, a male or female caregiver, but we didn't use those words; instead it was kind of half-Czech, *betreuerka*. The ending of the word is Czech.

How did things run in the camp at Terezín?

In Terezín all the orders came from the Germans; the head was a *Lagerkommandant*, and then there were some others under him. They could come round for checks at any time. We never knew when it was going to be. But internal order-keeping was divided. There were Czech gendarmes who kept watch over us; they were by and large decent and in many cases they tried to help us. For example, they would help smuggle various letters or packages out, and for that goodwill, of course, many of them paid with their lives. So those were the Czech gendarmes, who were on watch at all the entry gates. When we went to work, they would do pocket searches, count us again – how many left, how many arrived – that was their job. And there were other elements, because in Terezín they set up so-called self-governance. By the Jews.

So the Betreuers, Heimleiters, *they were all . . .?*

They were all part of the Jewish self-governing body. And at the most local level, order was kept by the *Ghettowache*.

Yes, who you called the get'áci. *And they were also Jews.*

Yes, of course. *Ghettowache*, shortened in Czech to *get'áci*. That's more Terezín slang, which you need to understand. The *Ghettowache* didn't specifically have uniforms – but they did have caps

[192]

– sort of round, black ones with a yellow stripe; they had a belt and strap. I drew it in several pictures [see 'Children Go to Lessons' in the colour inset].

Could you tell me a bit about what happened to you after the war?

For a long time there was no interest in what happened afterwards. People thought: the war has ended and everything's OK. Of course it wasn't at all, and that's another era that needs to be recorded; it's only recently that people have started to ask what happened after the war was over. My mother and I returned from Mauthausen on 29 May [1945]. We arrived in the middle of the night, they let us sleep somewhere and in the morning they told us: 'You're free, go home.' And there was nowhere to go. And that's how it began.

So how did you find a place to live?

We had nowhere to go. So the first place we went was to our old neighbours, who lived next door to us in our building, and who had behaved very decently to us, even during the war. And that was the address – I think all Jewish families did this – where we'd said to each other: after the war we'll meet here. So the first thing we did was go to them. Their name was Pěchoč. And of course they invited us in, welcomed us, let us sleep on their feather beds and gave us white coffee and rolls the next morning for breakfast. We were so weakened that we couldn't eat anything rich. Sometimes people gave the returnees a huge meal and it cost them their lives. They announced that everywhere on the radio, so people would know not to do it.

But the interesting thing is, we'd survived everything, and

your body will hold out just as long as it has to. And now that everything was over it just gave out: we stayed there one day and got a fever. Everywhere there were announcements that the people who were returning from the camps had typhus, so they took us to the typhus ward. So I ended up being treated for typhus. That family had a grocery shop, so we caused them a lot of unpleasantness, because after we left they had to have everything disinfected, the shop and so forth.

They released me from the hospital before my mum. I didn't want to burden the Pěchoč family any more, but I had no place to go. We literally walked the streets looking for somewhere to sleep. There were some shelters where they would let us stay the night, but only ever one night, I don't know why. So each morning we'd walk round trying to find somewhere to sleep that night. And various charities would cook meals for people in certain places, so each morning we'd go to Wilson Station, where they made coffee and gave us a bit of bread or something. And we'd carry it in our hands – we didn't have a bag, or money, or anything. At noon there'd be soup somewhere else, so we'd go and have some soup, and then sleep in one of the shelters.

So the beginning was very difficult. Then they released my mum, and then there was another shelter where we lived for a week or so. Then we started to look for a flat and that was quite complicated.

This was the flat I left to go to Terezín; I was born in this flat. This was what we left when we were deported. But when Jews abandoned their flats, the first thing that happened was that the flats were emptied; they carted away everything that was there, put it into various warehouses and allocated the flat to a German. And that German would then go to the warehouses and requisi-

[194]

tion some furnishings. So a German lived here during the war; his name was Otto Werner. The only thing that remained of his in the flat [when he left] was a brass plaque he had on the door with his name on it: he did take it off the door, but it stayed in the flat. In those revolutionary days [in May 1945] he fled – I heard he left on a bicycle – but he gave the apartment keys to the building manager; he was at least decent enough to do that. And people were terribly curious: they must have thought everything here belonged to the Germans, so people from the building piled into the flat and took what they could, and . . . well, it was complicated.

But in the end you got your flat back.

We got the flat back some time that summer; we were somewhere in a convalescent facility. In September I started school. I was fifteen and a half, and my last education in a school had been in Year 5 of primary school.

So you went to the academic high school, the gymnázium . . .

I started in Year 4 of secondary school, the *kvarta*. I should have been in *kvinta*, Year 5, but I went one year back and belatedly took the entrance exam.

And from there you went . . . ?

Well, I wanted to paint. So I transferred to a different high school, but it was a school of graphic design, a technical school. The subjects were mostly technical in nature and I regretted not having a more rounded education. So I went to that school during the day and did the academic course at the *gymnázium* as an external student. And after four years of that, I did two sets of school-leaving exams: at the graphics school and at the academic high school.

And was it then that you decided to make painting your career?

I decided then that it would be my profession, so I took the entrance exams for the Academy of Arts, Architecture and Design [in Prague]. But even that wasn't so simple.

Tell me about when you got your diary back.

Yes, I'd been lucky, because my uncle actually was in that one profession in Terezín that was basically indispensable: he worked in the records department. So he had access to all the documents, which he hid, and then after the war he and Dr Lagus even published a book using them. I think it's one of the best books about Terezín to come out, because it has all the facts from those documents. Even today, when I need to check something, I can find it in that book. It's called *Město za mřížemi* [*City behind Bars*].

He hid those documents, and because I knew worse things were coming, fortunately I didn't take my diary or my drawings with me. Before I left for Auschwitz I gave them to him. And he hid them together with his documents; he bricked them into a wall in Magdeburg barracks.

It was his occupation that protected him. He managed to shield his wife as well. After the war he went back [to Terezín]; he knew where he'd hidden them. So he removed them and brought them to me.

At that point you had your papers and drawings back; what happened with them?

What happened? Not much of anything. Now and then an article would come out somewhere. I think I told them at the [State Jewish] museum that I had the diary. A bit of it came out in English. And also in 1960 or thereabouts there was one publisher, Naše vojsko [Our Armed Forces], who put out a book called *Deníky dětí* [*Children's Diaries*]. A bit of it was published there, in Czech. But that was heavily edited, shortened – I might even have done that myself, because I knew only a bit of it would be published, so I cut it down.

In general, what was the attitude in post-war Czechoslovakia towards Jews and their wartime experiences?

Well, it varied, of course. First of all, no one had figured on us returning. And when we did, it was rather a surprise for people. We threw them. They'd say: 'Wow, so you've come back? Who would ever have thought?' And 'What a shame that your dad didn't come back as well.' That's the sort of reactions they had. And then they'd start to say: 'Don't think we had it easy or anything; we were hungry too.' And they'd start to tell us their stories, which seemed completely ludicrous to us. Because their hunger was nothing compared to our hunger and their difficulties were laughable.

So people weren't very interested in it. We'd even hidden some of our things with these people. We could only take 50 kilograms of luggage with us; we had to leave the rest of it in our flat and even hand in a list of what we were leaving. People tried to hide a few things with Aryans they knew – the removal of the Jews was called

Aryanization, because there were 'Aryans' and 'non-Aryans'; we were the 'non-Aryans' and they were the 'Aryans' – and the results were varied. Some of the Aryans behaved quite awfully. We were rather lucky to get our things back. Not all of them, of course: I remember that one woman said a ring of ours had rolled away from them in the loft. Or my mum had exchanged her gold watch for a chrome one before we left, so she'd be allowed to take it with her, although in the end she had to give it up anyway. And those people told us: 'You have to understand – it was wartime and there was nothing to eat, so we traded it for some lard.' Or something like that. So we had a little of that too, but it happened to a lot of Jews that people denied them their things and didn't return them.

And then came 1948, the Communist coup.

Yes, that was a bad year. The situation for Jews here was pretty ugly.

And I assume the end of the 1940s and the beginning of the 1950s were too?

Yes, they were. You're probably thinking of the Slánský trials. That was a truly bad time. At the time I was going to the Academy of Arts. My original professor, Mr Fila, who taught monumental painting, which is what I was studying, unfortunately died while I was in my second year. So they divided us up between the other studios. That's how I got into the studio of Antonín Pelc, who taught political caricature. No one there tried to force me to do caricatures, because they'd taken me in from another department, but what the students there were doing . . . those were awful things. And it was very anti-Semitic;

that whole trial was anti-Semitic. Ninety per cent of the accused were Jewish. They hadn't even been religious, they had been Communists, but each of them had to start his confession with the words: 'I, of Jewish origin . . .' And they said it. What things they must have done to make them . . . It was a terrible time.

So when was there renewed interest in your story? Maybe the 1960s? I'm assuming that while there were various trials against 'cosmopolitans' going on, no one would want to talk much about the war, or at least about the Jews' experiences.

True, but that was the whole Communist regime – it just was that way.

Sort of contradictory, almost . . .

And then came '68. But a bit before then the situation loosened up a little. There were good relations originally between Czechoslovakia and Israel. In Israel they remember it even today, because Czechoslovakia helped them at the time; they even trained Israeli soldiers here as pilots. Relations were so good at the time that a scholarship was offered for one Czech artist to spend ten weeks in Israel and I got it. It was the most beautiful time of my life. I even changed my whole style of painting – we haven't spoken much about that, but you can read about it elsewhere. When I returned, I put together an exhibition from the sketches I'd brought back; it was very successful. I had invitations from abroad to mount exhibitions – and then came August '68 and the gate slammed shut. The end of everything for twenty more years.

But still, you stayed here that whole time, when many Jews emigrated to various countries.

Yes, a large number of those who came back and particularly the young ones, those few who survived, emigrated right after the war. They went to various places: to the US or wherever they had relatives who'd left in time. Whereas here they'd lost their whole family – young people, my age, for example, by themselves – so their families abroad invited them and took them in. So some emigrated to their relatives and those who had nowhere to go went to Israel. They volunteered for the [Israeli] army, the Haganah – that was right after the war. I wanted to do that too. I was in contact with them, but I don't know – maybe it was just an excuse on my part. I wanted to go, but I was just a bit afraid. I'm not the brave type for emigration, but on the other hand – and this was one of my main reasons – my mum was here and she didn't dare go. And to leave my mother behind was just out of the question. So I stayed.

Various political and cultural periods have come and gone here, and I'm interested to know whether your own opinions about your experiences and your diary have changed over that time as well.

My whole artistic oeuvre depicts my life. And in it you can read everything about me.

First I finished my course, then I did various studies, sketches and normal drawings, and then in the 1960s I started to come to terms with my past. I painted the Holocaust; I think I wanted to do something like Goya did, *The Disasters of War*. But then in '64 I wanted to finish with that and I told myself: 'I've painted that now, that's the end.'

Then I got that scholarship to Israel and there everything changed. Suddenly it was optimism and sun, and the colours all changed, and so forth. Then came '68 and I stopped painting completely for a few years, because I didn't want to paint war any more and I couldn't paint what I wanted to. Because suddenly everything was anti-Israeli. Even at that exhibition I had, I was cautious enough not to mention Israel. It was called *Travels in the Holy Land*. Because by then even the word 'Israel' had become dangerous, and later it was completely taboo. I didn't want more war, I couldn't paint Israel, so for a few years I just stopped painting altogether.

Then I finally went to do something I had never wanted to do, even though I had the qualifications for it: I started to teach. I taught at a people's art school. Originally I just went to stand in for a colleague who said it would be for two months. Then she went to Switzerland and wrote that she wasn't coming back; she emigrated. I stayed at that school for fourteen years. For a few years I didn't paint; then I started going back to it, but it wasn't about Israel any more. Or there were a few reminiscences about Israel, but it was more about the Holocaust again, although not exactly. It was more like war in general and everything I'd lived through. Another cycle of paintings came out of it called *Devastations*. And in it are paintings like 'Overturned Roots', 'Wounded Earth', 'Devastation', and so forth. You can read everything from those paintings, the way life was then.

What did people say in those days about Terezín and the Holocaust?

People didn't talk about Terezín at all. There are two fortresses in the town: the main fortress and the small fortress. The small fortress was always a political prison. Then it was a Gestapo prison. And they turned the large fortress, where the town was, into the ghetto. There's a national cemetery in the small fortress and they would celebrate various days of remembrance there. But no one spoke about Terezín. Even the building where the museum is today: there was a plan to make it into a museum of the ghetto even back then, but they wouldn't approve it. They turned it into a Museum of the National Security Forces. And when, for instance, people from as far away as America would come here, wanting to see where their parents had died, they'd ride through Terezín and say: 'Yes, we've been there, there was nothing there anyway.' So Terezín was hushed up.

After the war, they wrote the names of all the people who'd perished on [the walls of] the Pinkas Synagogue. Then, under the Socialists, they said that the building needed repair, put up scaffolding all around it and the 'reconstruction work' lasted forty years. It was inaccessible. And only after the revolution, in 1990, did they take the scaffolding down and rewrite all the names there. So that's what the situation looked like. Terezín wasn't there, the names weren't there. I think it's important you know about this; it says quite a lot about the times.

So the synagogue was like that the whole time from 1948 until 1989?

Yes, it was surrounded by scaffolding and 'under reconstruction'.

I think I remember that from when I was here shortly before the revolution in 1989.

So you'll remember what it looked like; there was construction all around it. But that just wasn't the case. They just took down the names and put up scaffolding.

Could you tell me something about your family now?

I got married while I was studying at the art academy. And in my second to last year, I gave birth prematurely to twins, but one of them died the day after. So I had to break off my studies for a year and finish up later. And four years after that my daughter was born.

So I have a son and a daughter. My son is a well-known musician, a cellist; he's on the senior staff at the Music Academy in Prague. His daughter, my granddaughter Dominika, is a top-flight solo cellist. She studied for two years in Israel and one of her main focuses is Jewish music. She's even managed to really bring me back to Judaism, so that subject has reappeared in my more recent work now. I do keep going back to the war as well, of course, but that also involves Jewish themes.

My husband was a musician too, a bass player and member of the Czechoslovak Radio Symphony Orchestra. And one other granddaughter, Dominika's sister, has gone in the other direction and is studying fine art. It stays in the family.

So you have three generations of artists . . .

It was slightly more complicated than that, because we had a mixed marriage. My husband was even from a very devout Catholic family, but nonetheless we had a great deal of mutual respect. Because religion was repressed here during Communism, his family was persecuted for their Catholicism. His brother was in prison for thirteen years; my sister-in-law did about twelve, another brother-in-law three and a half. So my whole life I was involved with prisons. I think that's also important to know.

Over the past sixty years a large number of memoirs have been published about the Holocaust; films have been made about people's experiences.

A lot of things have come out. Not all of them are good; some are even very bad. And some distort matters; there's misinformation, things that didn't happen or even couldn't have happened . . .

Human memory is a strange thing.

But it's not even about memory. In places it can be intentional. An intention to hush up certain things or pass over them, not to speak of some things and to exaggerate others . . .

It's difficult to film things of this sort. Every book or every film has within it the personal experience of the author. But it has to be truthful. And there are actually very few truthful ones. One of the best [people], who tells the truth, is, for example, Elie Wiesel, whose words I often quote when I'm interviewed – although I always make it clear that they're his words; I don't take them as my own. As far as Terezín goes, Ruth Bondy's book is a true account. She's originally from Prague but has lived in Israel for years; she wrote a book called *'Elder of the Jews': Jakob Edelstein of Theresienstadt*, so that's a good book. Then I read an excellent book by Imre Kertész called *Fateless*. So there are a few books like that, and then there are some that are utterly poor, fictitious, distorted.

What would you say is the contribution of your diary? Why should we read another account of the Holocaust?

Mostly because it is truthful. I've put my own sentiments into it as well, but those sentiments themselves are emotional, moving and most of all truthful. And maybe because it's narrated in that half-childish way, it's accessible and expressive, and I think it will help people to understand those times.

Notes

Helga's Diary

p. 7 'mobilization': On 23 September 1938, the Czechoslovak government declared a general mobilization for an impending state of war.

p. 7 all about Austria: A reference to the *Anschluss*, the annexation of Austria in 1938.

p. 7 I'll be nine soon: As mentioned in the Translator's Note, these first few entries were rewritten extensively by Helga after the war. They were probably composed at Terezín or shortly before, but, as might be expected, there is no mention of age in the original manuscript.

p. 9 Úvaly: Today a suburb of Prague on the eastern outskirts of the city.

p. 9 the Second Republic: The First Czechoslovak Republic existed from the declaration of independence in 1918 until Beneš's resignation in the wake of the Munich agreement of 1938 and the occupation of the Sudetenland by Germany. The Second Republic lasted only a few months thereafter, until the dismemberment of Czechoslovakia after the Nazi invasion in 1939.

p. 11 Aryan: The Nazis' term for members of superior 'races', typically depicted as light-skinned, light-haired Northern Europeans, who were favoured by German legislation and orders throughout the Nazi era. Jews were by definition non-Aryans.

p. 13 'Gestapo': Short for *Geheime Staatspolizei* or 'Secret State Police'. By the time Czechoslovakia was annexed, the Gestapo also included the security services and the criminal police; they were in charge of the incarceration, deportation and internment of the Jews.

p. 14 Autumn 1940: This date has been inserted to help the reader make sense of the timing.

p. 14 I passed my exam: According to Helga, the Jewish community in Prague organized exams for pupils who were being home-educated since they had been excluded from regular schooling.

p. 15 Summer 1941: This date has been inserted to help the reader make sense of the timing.

p. 19 A month has passed: The German Interior Minister's decree mandating that all Jews over the age of six wear yellow stars of David sewn to their clothing dates from 1 September 1941. This entry, despite its date, seems to cover events from early September to early October. Thus when Helga writes later 'A further month passed' (see below), she is actually only bringing us forward to early October (the date for the next entry is just a week later, on 12 October).

p. 21 A further month passed: The month referred to here is apparently between the decree (early September) and these events (early October).

p. 21 *transports*: This German term has been co-opted into both Czech and English to describe the forced deportation of the Jews and other 'undesirables' to the camps and other fates. Helga often uses it as well to refer to the trains that were usually used for this purpose.

p. 22 solid alcohol: A kind of fuel used for lighting or cooking; it comes in blocks or cakes.

p. 22 the shops would be closed: There is a slight discrepancy in the dates here as 12 October was a Sunday, but some of the references ('Last night', 'Tomorrow') seem to be written from the point of view of Saturday.

p. 22 'Trade Fair': Alternately referred to here as *Veletrh* or 'Trade Fair' and *Veletržní palác* or 'Trade Fair Palace', this grand exhibition hall for hosting trade fairs was built in 1929 in Prague's Holešovice district. Jews reported to the nearby *Rádiotrh*, 'Radio Market', to be processed and housed during deportation proceedings. (These run-down wooden barracks have since been demolished.) According to Helga, people referred to the whole area as *Veletrh*, which is reflected in her usage.

p. 23 in it: Helga writes of people being 'in it' or 'not in it', by which she means ordered to report for deportation or not.

p. 29 Střešovice: District of Prague where the headquarters of the Centre for Jewish Deportations (later renamed the Central Office for the Resolution of the Jewish Question in Bohemia and Moravia) was located. All Jews had to undergo processing here in advance of the transports.

p. 30 AK (*Aufbaukommando*): The first construction squad (the 'construction commandos'), which was sent to make Terezín ready for the influx of new inhabitants, the AK formed part of the highest 'caste' of Terezín society (see page 182 for more details).

p. 30 4 December 1941: This entry starts with events several days before this; the date specified is the Thursday on which they had to go to sign up.

p. 31 rear carriage: Remember that – as Helga said earlier – Jews had to ride in a specially designated rear carriage of the tram. If there was only one carriage, they had to wait for the next tram.

p. 35 The Trade Fair Palace is swarming with people: Here Helga evidently means the Radio Market; in the original manuscript it does not say what building they were in, and the specific mention was evidently added later, erroneously.

p. 44 his count: The *Ordners* were Jews, hence they were both wardens and prisoners. His count (Helga calls it the *Standt*) was the number of Jews under his watch.

p. 44 Říp: An odd-shaped hill that sticks straight out of the flat, central Bohemian plain. Legend has it that the forefather of the Czech nation climbed the hill, liked what he saw and decided to settle his tribe here. Říp's distinctive shape is recognizable to every Czech schoolchild.

p. 45 Sudetenland: Many of the barracks at Terezín were named after cities or places in the Third Reich (Sudetenland, Dresden, Magdeburg, Hamburg, etc.)

p. 45 AK: Short for *Aufbaukommando* (see note on page 209).

p. 52 men's brigade: Movement around Terezín was strictly

controlled and normally the Jews were only allowed out in organized groups, typically for work purposes. I have called these groups 'brigades'; Helga uses the Czech word *kolona*, borrowed from the German *Kolonne*.

p. 52 they'll come here as well: Helga means that her father will be sent over in a group of Jews to carry suitcases.

p. 53 'coincidentally': See page 192, where Helga talks about the small kindnesses shown to them by some of the Czech gendarmes.

p. 61 in the *Schleuse*: Literally 'in the sluice', this was the process upon entry to and exit from the camp during which the Germans divested the Jews of their possessions and valuables. In this meaning it is specific to Terezín and even gets borrowed into Czech in the form *šlojska* (as Helga explains on page 189).

p. 62 in the office: Helga's father worked in the finance office (*Wirtschaftsabteilung*) at Terezín.

p. 63 'sluice' it: The Terezín Jews also used the term *Schleuse* as a verb, meaning 'to scrounge' (Czech *šlojzovat*). In their view this was distinct from *stealing*; it was more like *lifting* something, as no disapproval accrued to taking from one's captors (as Helga explains on page 189).

p. 64 '*Toranuth*': Sometimes written *Toranut*, this is a Hebrew term.

p. 66 only the Vrbas are missing: The Vrbas were close relatives – Helga's mother's sister and her family.

p. 67 *The Bartered Bride*: An opera by Czech composer Bedřich

Smetana. The premiere took place on 28 November 1942. Helga at a later point inserted this extra line into the manuscript; it works thematically, but comes several months too early.

p. 70 I wouldn't move out of here now: These two paragraphs appear to have been written later, as they are not in Helga's original manuscript. The mention of *The Kiss* is even later, as it is handwritten into a post-war typescript. Although Helga did see this production, she could not have done so until after the premiere in July 1943, so the mention here is thematic rather than chronological.

p. 70 Čapek's *First Team, R.U.R., The Mother*: Three works by Czech author Karel Čapek.

p. 70 *The Kiss*: Another opera by Bedřich Smetana.

p. 72 *Altertransports*: Chronologically this passage belongs at this point in the manuscript, although Helga clearly did not write it this way originally; it is on a separate page, in a different and later hand. The maturity of the style here suggests this might have been written after the war as she was recalling the rest of her experiences.

p. 75 Three young lads escaped: This passage was written on a separate sheet of paper in a much later hand, so its place in the manuscript is unclear. There was a similar event in Terezín that occurred in April 1943, but the mention of 'winter' seems to contradict that, so this passage has been left where Helga put it originally.

p. 76 With so few opportunities for amusement: We have removed a sentence just before this that was added during a later edit and is clearly an error. The sentence it replaced is unreadable in the original pages and could not be reconstructed.

p. 76 mixed-race girls: In Nazi Germany, Jews and Aryans were considered different races. Here, then, Helga means that one parent was Christian and the other Jewish.

p. 76 Chanukah is before Christmas: The Jewish Festival of Lights has a fixed date in the Jewish calendar. In the Christian calendar it comes at varying points in December, often quite close to Christmas. Chanukah involves a festive meal and the lighting of the *chanukiah*, a nine-branched *menorah* or candelabra.

p. 76 poor-man's cream: From the Czech Yiddish *daleskrém*; Helga says this was made by whipping water with sugar in it.

p. 77 14 days after the New Year: This date appears in the loose-leaf pages, but without the year. Helga has reconstructed it as being 1943, which matches both with the information about the transport (which took place on 20 January 1943) and the typhus epidemic, which peaked in February 1943.

p. 79 Shops are opening: These three paragraphs are written together in a later hand on a separate sheet of paper; we have inserted them here because the mention of *Ghettogeld* is tied clearly to May 1943, when this scrip was introduced in Terezín.

p. 79 *Ghettogeld*: Scrip printed for the residents of Terezín to use in the camp's shops.

p. 81 to pick spinach: Kréta was an area on the edge of the ghetto used at the time as a garden for the camp.

p. 81 A lecture on Rembrandt: These two paragraphs are not in the original manuscript and Helga must have added them later, after the war.

p. 81 'I'm dying of thirst . . .': The Villon translation is taken from http://www.poetryintranslation.com/PITBR/French/Villon.htm. Translated by A. S. Kline © 2004 All Rights Reserved. Reproduced here by permission of A. S. Kline.

p. 85 the Sokol hall: An early Czech version of the Boy Scouts, focusing on patriotism and exercise.

p. 85 *Entwesung*: Helga frequently uses this word, which in German refers to pest control. The Czech equivalent that also crops up in her diaries, *desinfekce*, 'disinfection', is somewhat broader in meaning.

p. 86 And that horrible, inexplicable rumour – gas!: The Polish children arrived in Terezín during the summer of 1943 and were deported to Auschwitz in October. This entry is therefore thematic, overlapping with the previous one, and appears to have been written later, perhaps after Helga realized the significance of their arrival and subsequent deportation.

p. 89 the rest found *Notbelags*: In other words, they found places to sleep up in the lofts or between other bunks.

p. 90 The Chanukah celebration begins: This description is closely associated in Helga's mind with the drawing 'Chanukah in the Loft', which is dated 16 January 1944. In 1943 Chanukah fell shortly before Christmas, and just after the 18 December transport that took away many of Helga's friends and relatives; this is referred to in the preceding paragraph.

p. 90 *Heimleiter*: The warden was part of the *samospráva* or self-governing apparatus of the Jewish community within Terezín.

p. 90 *'Ma'oz tzur yeshu'ati . . .'*: The opening words of a traditional Chanukah song, sung in Hebrew after the lighting of the candles.

p. 91 Burgr: Helga evidently spelled this name the way she heard it. He himself spelled it Burger.

p. 92 encephalitis: The epidemic peaked in December 1943, and the moving of Hamburg barracks took place in January 1944.

p. 93 Hora's poems: Josef Hora was a Czech poet of the early twentieth century. Pictures of Helga's copybook can be found in the photographic inset. Helga apparently added this passage later, as it is not in the original manuscript.

p. 94 Hradčany and the River Vltava: Hradčany is the famous castle in Prague and the River Vltava runs just at its foot.

p. 94 a general review: Helga thinks this was not about the Red Cross committee that visited later in 1944; it probably concerned a preparatory visit by the Germans. The Red Cross visit is described further along in the text.

p. 94 the wishing-table: The Brothers Grimm fairy tale 'The Wishing-table, the Golden Ass and the Cudgel in the Sack' is a favourite in the Czech lands, although less well known in Anglo-Saxon countries. The wishing-table can make a magnificent feast appear magically.

p. 95 *'Zum Park'*, *'Zum Bad'*: 'To the Park', 'To the Baths'.

p. 95 *Glimmer*: Processing of the mineral mica (used in German aeroplane manufacture).

p. 96 Danish hostels: Approximately 500 Danish Jews were deported to Terezín. Their presence there was one of the prime motivators for the Red Cross visit that caused all this sudden renovation.

p. 96 instead of celebrating Mother's Day: Mother's Day was traditionally celebrated on the second Sunday in May – in this case, 14 May 1944.

p. 96 those few dozen grams: Throughout her manuscript, Helga uses decagrams (units of ten grams), a common Czech measure for foodstuffs; we have converted these to grams to aid the non-Czech reader.

p. 98 Voskovec and Werich: A popular Czech variety act with Prague's Liberated Theatre (*Osvobozené divadlo*), starting in 1927. They quickly came into conflict with the Nazi regime and emigrated to the USA in 1939, returning after the war was over.

p. 102 'Uncle Rahm': Karl Rahm was the *Gruppenführer* (commandant) of Terezín for the SS. Other eyewitness testimonies also recall how he made children address him as 'Onkel Rahm' in front of the Red Cross committee.

p. 105 Lípa: A small village near Havlíčkův Brod, in the eastern part of Bohemia.

p. 106 the *Toranut* girls: The Hebrew word *Toranut* is used here of chores done for others or for the common good.

p. 106 'as nosy as a bedbug': A Czech phrase (*dotěrná jako štěnice*).

p. 108 Rosh Hashanah: The Jewish New Year has a fixed date in the Jewish calendar, which usually falls in September in the Christian calendar. In Judaism, the 'day' starts at sundown, so the holiday starts on the evening of the previous day.

p. 110 Yom Kippur: The Jewish Day of Atonement falls ten days after the New Year and is marked with a day-long fast.

p. 113 *Manon Lescaut*: Czech poet Vítězslav Nezval wrote a verse play in 1940 based on the novel by Abbé Prévost.

p. 116 a new notebook: This does not correspond to any surviving notebook or loose-leaf pages. In any event, anything Helga had taken with her from Terezín would have been confiscated upon arrival at Auschwitz-Birkenau and lost. This and all subsequent entries were written after her return to Prague in 1945.

p. 119 Birkenau, the work camp: Birkenau was in fact not a work camp, but Helga said they discovered this only later (see the interview with her on page 184).

p. 126 *Lagerruhe*: According to Helga, during camp curfew inmates were required to lie on their bunks and keep quiet. Any activity or movement was forbidden.

p. 137 28 October: Helga was referring here to the national holiday commemorating Czechoslovak independence in 1918.

p. 137 Šára . . . Uša: The first bit of each of these nicknames sounds in Czech like part of the German *Unterscharführer*. Not only were they conveniently shorter, but they offered the added bonus that any Germans overhearing them would not know who was being spoken about.

p. 146 Flossenbürg: The main concentration camp to which Freiberg, a satellite work camp, was affiliated.

p. 150 Most . . . Chomutov: These northern Czech towns and the rest of the border area, called the Sudetenland, were annexed to the Reich at the start of the war. Their populations were mixed German and Czech.

p. 151 Triebschitz: A work camp just outside Most.

pp. 153–4 Stalin candles: The Soviets dropped magnesium flare bombs to illuminate the terrain below them at night, improving their bombing accuracy. These commonly went by the name 'Stalin candles'.

p. 171 'Wienergraben': A quarry belonging to Mauthausen concentration camp.

Interview with Helga Weiss

p. 185 Jakob Edelstein: served as *Judenälteste* (Elder of the Jews) from 1941 to 1943 and as the Deputy to the *Judenälteste* from January to December 1943, when he was deported to Auschwitz. Edelstein and his family were executed in June 1944.

p. 194 We literally walked: 'We' here refers to Helga and her aunt, who had also been released from quarantine at the same time.

p. 195 entrance exam: At the time Helga went to school, Czech children attended a primary school for five years, after which they could take entrance exams for further schooling. Two of the possibilities were a technical high school, which prepared them for a trade or entrance into a technical college, or a *gymnázium*, an academic high school preparing them for entrance to a university. *Gymnázium* lasted eight years; the years had Latin-derived names, so *kvarta* was the fourth year of study and *kvinta* was the fifth year.

p. 196 *Město za mřížemi*: Karel Lagus served as curator of the State Jewish Museum in Prague and was on the board of directors of the Terezín Memorial. He had spent the war years in Terezín alongside Helga's uncle, Josef Polák; their book was published in 1962. It has not been translated into English.

p. 197 came out in English: Excerpts from Helga's diary were published in *Terezín*, edited by František Ehrmann, Otta Heitlinger and Rudolf Iltis (Council of Jewish Communities in the Czech Lands, Prague, 1965), pp. 106–9.

p. 198 Slánský trials: A series of purge trials within the Czechoslovak Communist Party in the early 1950s, starting with the eminent Party member Rudolf Slánský. As Helga says, most of the accused were Jewish and they were said to have been 'cosmopolitans', a code word for bourgeois Jews or Zionists. They were forced to recant their supposed infractions and eleven of the fourteen tried were put to death.

p. 199 '68: After a few years of growing liberalization in Czechoslovakia, in early 1968 Communist Party Secretary Alexander Dubček announced that there would be further loosening of controls on freedom of speech and economic activity and increasing democratization. This brief experiment in 'socialism with a human face', known as the Prague Spring, ended in August of that same year, when Warsaw Pact troops, acting on orders from Moscow, invaded Czechoslovakia and re-established tighter controls.

Glossary

Although Helga came from a Czech-speaking Jewish family and began her life in the independent Czechoslovak state, where Czech was the first official language, the imposition of Nazi rule and, later, life at the camps meant that the presence of German loomed ever larger in her world. She refers to many places and events by their German names, frequently adapted into Czech and conjugated or declined as a Czech word would be. These words have been 'translated' into English in a similar way, to ensure that the English reader has the flavour of her text in the same way that a Czech reader would. Helga also occasionally uses words from Yiddish or Hebrew, but these are explained in the text or notes and do not appear in this glossary.

Achtung	*warning, attention*
alle heraus	*everybody out*
alles da lassen	*leave everything where it is*
Altertransport	*deportation of the elderly*
Arbeitslager	*work camp*
Aufbaukommando	*construction squad*
Aufseher	*overseer*
Bahnbau	*railway construction*
Bauhof	*yard*
Betreuer, Betreuerin	*caregiver*

Bettrolle	bedrolls
Damen und Herrenlatrinen	women's and men's WCs
Entwesung	disinfestation
Ferien	holidays
Häftlingsnummer	prisoner number
Handgepäck	hand luggage
Heim	home, house
Heimleiter	warden (in Terezín)
heraus	(get) out
Hilfsdienst	volunteer unit
Hochalarm	red alert
Infektionsgefahr	risk of infection
Jude	Jew
Jugendfürsorge	child welfare
Jugendheim	boys' home
Kaffeehaus	coffee house
Kasernensperre	curfew, confinement to quarters
Kinderheim	children's home
Knaben und Mädchenschule	boys' and girls' school
Kommandatur	camp headquarters
Krankenlager	sickbed
Krankenträger	stretcher-bearer
Kriechlingsheim	toddlers' home
Lagerkommandant	camp commander
Lagerruhe	silence in the camp, camp curfew
Landwirtschaft	agriculture department
Lehrlingsheim	apprentices' home
Leichenwagen	hearse
Lichtsperre	blackout

Mädchenheim	girls' home
Mänerlager	men's camp
Nachschub	extra portion
Nachtrage	latecomers
Notbelag	emergency billet – i.e. sleeping in lofts or between bunks
Ordner	marshal
Posten	sentry
Putzkolonne	cleaning brigade
Raumwirtschaft	space management department
rechts	to the right
ruhe	silence, quiet
Salmeister	workroom manager
Säuglingsheim	infants' home
Schleuse	'the sluice', a name for the camp entry and departure process, in which Jews were systematically shaken down for any valuable possessions
schneller	hurry up
Schupo	state police
Speisehalle	dining hall
Standt	attendance
stehen bleiben	stay put, halt
Tagesbefehl	daily orders
Transport	deportation and also the trains used in the process
Transportleiter	deportation manager
Transportleitung	deportation administration
Übersiedlungschein	relocation ticket
Unterscharführer	sergeant

Verschönerung der Stadt	*beautification of the town*
Voralarm	*advance alarm*
Waisenkind	*orphan*
Waschraum	*washroom*
Zimmerälteste	*room's elder*
Zimmertour	*room duty*
Zulag	*bonus*
Zum Bad	*to the baths*
Zum Park	*to the park*
Zusatz	*supplement*

Illustration Credits

All paintings and drawings are by Helga Weiss. © Wallstein Verlag, Germany, 1998. All rights reserved.

Facsimile of pages from Helga Weiss's diaries reproduced by permission of the author.

Photographs within the diary: page 12, © bpk; page 21, Jewish Museum Prague / Yad Vashem Archive; page 122, Courtesy of Yad Vashem Archive; page 177, United States Holocaust Memorial Museum / Yad Vashem Archive. Courtesy of Olga Fierzova. © United States Holocaust Memorial Museum.

Photographs in the plate section are used by permission of the author unless stated otherwise: page 2, bottom, akg-images / ullstein bild; page 3, top, Courtesy of Yad Vashem Archive; middle, Jewish Museum Prague / Yad Vashem Archive; bottom, Courtesy of Yad Vashem Archive; page 4, top, United States Holocaust Memorial Museum / Czechoslovak News Agency / Pamatnik Terezin nardoni kulturni pamatka. Courtesy of Ivan Vojtech Fric. © United States Holocaust Memorial Museum; bottom, United States Holocaust Memorial Museum / Czechoslovak News Agency / Pamatnik Terezin nardoni kulturni pamatka. Courtesy of Ivan Vojtech Fric. © United States

Tatínkovi se jim skutečně brání. Nastupujeme
do elektriky. Vůz je úplně prázdný. Vždyť je
sotva čtvrtě na šest. Jsou zde jen několik
dělníků, jedoucích do práce. Ale čím více
se blížíme ku oubrání práce, tím se včírák
plní nabalenými cestujícími. Vůz, do ně-
hož přestupujeme několik stanic od veletrhu, je již úplně přecpán. Jsme nuceni zů-
stat na plošině. "Veletržní palác", hlásí prů-
vodčí. Vůz se naráz vyprazdňuje. Ale ven se
tlačí všechny, jinaše cesta. Podél veletrhu stojí
nepřehledná řada čekajících lidí, do které
se také my stavíme. Řada se jen pomalu
pohybuje a přece bychom si přáli, aby se
nehýbala vůbec. Každým pohybem jsme
blíže k okamžiku, kdy si musíme dát

...línkové se jim ztěžka brání. Nastupujeme

do elektriky. Vůz je úplně prázdný. Vždyť je

...dva čtvrtě na šest. Je zde jen několik

dělníků, jedoucích do práce. Ale čím více

se blížíme ku vnitřní Praze, tím se vozňák

...ný nacpaný mi cestujícími. Vůz, do ně-

...ož přistupujeme několik stanic až velko-

...ka, je již úplně přecpán. Jsme nuceni zů-

stat na plošině. "Veletržní palác", hlásí prů-

vodčí. Vůz se naráz vyprazdňuje. Ale sem smě-

...řují všechny, jinak cesta. Před veletrhem stojí

nepřehledná řada, čekajících lidí, do které

se také my stavíme. Řada se jen pomalu

pohybuje a přece bychom si přáli, aby se

nehýbala vůbec. Každým pohybem jsme

blíže k okénku, kdy si musíme dát

He just wanted a decent book to read ...

Not too much to ask, is it? It was in 1935 when Allen Lane, Managing Director of Bodley Head Publishers, stood on a platform at Exeter railway station looking for something good to read on his journey back to London. His choice was limited to popular magazines and poor-quality paperbacks – the same choice faced every day by the vast majority of readers, few of whom could afford hardbacks. Lane's disappointment and subsequent anger at the range of books generally available led him to found a company – and change the world.

'We believed in the existence in this country of a vast reading public for intelligent books at a low price, and staked everything on it'
Sir Allen Lane, 1902–1970, founder of Penguin Books

The quality paperback had arrived – and not just in bookshops. Lane was adamant that his Penguins should appear in chain stores and tobacconists, and should cost no more than a packet of cigarettes.

Reading habits (and cigarette prices) have changed since 1935, but Penguin still believes in publishing the best books for everybody to enjoy. We still believe that good design costs no more than bad design, and we still believe that quality books published passionately and responsibly make the world a better place.

So wherever you see the little bird – whether it's on a piece of prize-winning literary fiction or a celebrity autobiography, political tour de force or historical masterpiece, a serial-killer thriller, reference book, world classic or a piece of pure escapism – you can bet that it represents the very best that the genre has to offer.

Whatever you like to read – trust Penguin.

read more
www.penguin.co.uk